Multiple Intelligences and Instructional Technology

Second Edition

Walter McKenzie

International Society for Technology in Education

EUGENE, OREGON • WASHINGTON, DC

Multiple Intelligences and Instructional Technology
SECOND EDITION

Walter McKenzie

Director of Publishing
Jean Marie Hall

Acquisitions Editor
Scott Harter

Production Editor
Tracy Cozzens

Production Coordinator
Amy Miller

Copy Editor
Lynne Ertle

Book Design and Layout
Kim McGovern

Cover Design
Signe Landin

Second Edition
ISBN 978-1-56484-188-9

Printed in the United States of America

International Society for Technology in Education (ISTE)
Washington, DC, Office:
    1710 Rhode Island Ave. NW, Suite 900, Washington, DC 20036-3132
Eugene, Oregon, Office:
    180 West 8th Ave., Suite 300, Eugene, OR 97401–2916
Order Desk: 1.800.336.5191
Order Fax: 1.541.302.3778
Customer Service: orders@iste.org
Book Publishing: books@iste.org
Rights and Permissions: permissions@iste.org
Books Sales and Marketing: booksmarketing@iste.org
Web: www.iste.org

About ISTE

The International Society for Technology in Education (ISTE) is the trusted source for professional development, knowledge generation, advocacy, and leadership for innovation. A nonprofit membership association, ISTE provides leadership and service to improve teaching, learning, and school leadership by advancing the effective use of technology in PK–12 and teacher education.

Home of the National Educational Technology Standards (NETS), the Center for Applied Research in Educational Technology (CARET), and ISTE's annual conference (formerly known as the National Educational Computing Conference, or NECC), ISTE represents more than 100,000 professionals worldwide. We support our members with information, networking opportunities, and guidance as they face the challenge of transforming education. To find out more about these and other ISTE initiatives, visit our website at **www.iste.org**.

As part of our mission, ISTE Book Publishing works with experienced educators to develop and produce practical resources for classroom teachers, teacher educators, and technology leaders. Every manuscript we select for publication is carefully peer-reviewed and professionally edited. We value your feedback on this book and other ISTE products. E-mail us at **books@iste.org**.

About the Author

Walter McKenzie is a lifelong learner who has been incorporating technology and multiple intelligences theory into instruction over the past two decades. He hosts an education Web site entitled The One and Only Surfaquarium (**http://surfaqaurium.com**), which includes innovative teaching resources, multiple intelligence pages, newsletters, projects, and online courses. Walter has written and taught multiple intelligence courses online and has presented on multiple intelligences, technology integration, and creative education to school employees and conference audiences around the nation. He resides in Massachusetts with his wife, Carleen, and his children, Christopher and Mallory. There he serves as director of information systems for the Salem Public Schools.

Dedication

This book is dedicated to educators everywhere who are rising to meet the challenge of education in the Information Age. Special thanks to Sheryl Asen for her guidance as friend and editor, and to my family for providing me with the time and support to make this book a reality.

Contents

Illustrations

Preface

This second edition of *Multiple Intelligences and Instructional Technology* offers additional insights into the relationship between human intelligence, technology, and effective instruction. The title and subject matter derive, of course, from Dr. Howard Gardner's well-known theory of multiple intelligences (MI), first advanced more than 20 years ago and considerably elaborated and modified by Gardner and other researchers in the years since. Gardner's theory holds that each of the separate intelligences is a viable, distinct pathway to learning. They are "ways of knowing" that can operate independently and yet act in concert with even greater power. These intelligences are not to be confused with talents, gifts, aptitudes, or learning styles. Talents, gifts, and aptitudes connote abilities that are above and beyond the realm of simple human understanding, such as the ability to play a musical instrument well or set new records in athletic competitions. Learning styles, meanwhile, are fixed modes of understanding that a learner uses regardless of the instructional context. Intelligences are more than either of these. They are legitimate conduits of cognition that can be flexibly applied across the curriculum in varied contexts by all learners.

Although we each have all the intelligences, they are distributed uniquely in every one of us. Because of this, there is a tendency to want to label learners by specific intelligences. Gardner is adamantly opposed to this. He sees his theory as a way to empower learners, not to diagnose deficits and prescribe remediation. Therefore, we should avoid discussing "types" of learners and any suggestion that there are surefire methods of instruction or implements of technology that accommodate specific learner strengths. Analyzing an existing lesson plan or unit by intelligences is one thing, but once that analysis is done, we need to rebuild the instruction holistically and replace it in its curricular context before delivering it to students.

The teachers I meet around the country are generally very excited about the curricular possibilities of MI theory and instructional technology—and they are also full of questions. Many indicate that they are already familiar with the theory and are ready to learn ways to implement it systematically in the classroom. The aim of this book is to help teachers dig deeper and realize the implications of Gardner's theory for diversifying their teaching practices in the classroom. There remains a huge void between Gardner's vision and its successful implementation in instruction. It is my hope that this second edition will continue to help bridge this gap by offering concrete strategies for using MI theory and technology in the classroom. I hope you will be empowered by the ideas presented herein, and that you will in turn empower your students as lifelong learners!

Walter McKenzie

January 2005

CHAPTER 1

A New Theory of Learning

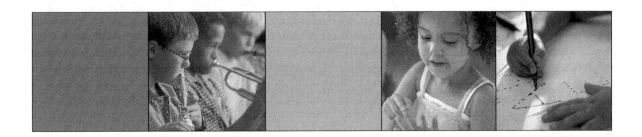

Ever since I was first introduced to Howard Gardner's theory of multiple intelligences (MI), my views of intelligence and instruction have changed. Where I once was trained to see learning deficits, I now recognize untapped potential. Old instructional practices have given way to new approaches to teaching and learning. It has become clear to me over time that, while Gardner was proposing a theory of intelligence, its best application in the classroom is as a learning theory. There are entirely new paths to learning, paths that have long gone unexplored. Along the way, many students have been left behind, unable to follow the traditional pathways to education.

A Letter From Paul

Consider a letter I received from Paul a couple of years ago. It touched me in a profound way, not unlike Gardner's work itself.

Dear Walter,

I am very glad I found your Web page (http://surfaquarium.com/MI/). We all would like to think we are smart. Could you help me with three problems I have? One, I think all the time, but noise like TV and radio distract me. Two, I can look at anything and see it in three dimensions. And three, I always am looking on things that relate in forms and genealogies. I want to believe I have some smarts. I am a dreamer, a visionary, a futurist, yet cannot use those talents to their fullest ability. I am 56 years old and retired. Do you think I am different than the "normal" crowd, and why? You answer is very important to me. Even if your answer is negative it cannot hurt my feelings.

—Paul

After some consideration of this heartfelt inquiry, I provided Paul with the following response:

Dear Paul,

Thanks for writing. Gardner stresses how culturally based intelligence is. What constitutes genius in the U.S. today is totally useless in Micronesia. The kinds of intelligence you have described to me are visual, naturalist, and logical. Visual and naturalist intelligences have not traditionally been valued in our society, and at 56 you probably had a hard row to hoe trying to find your niche in the middle of this century in our culture. It amazes me how much suffering people have had to endure because their mental strengths were not the ones schools or businesses emphasized. I can tell from the tone of your letter that you have felt troubled because of this tendency in our society.

The good news is that society is going through great change. Whereas visual thinkers used to be classified as artists and architects, and naturalists used to be labeled as environmentalists and academics, now someone of your abilities has options to realize his or her potential as a visionary—an idea person who thinks "outside the box." In my experience, visual thinkers are some of the most creative because they look at ideas in nontraditional, nonverbal ways. Likewise, naturalists are creative in that they organize and analyze things in ways that are different from the traditional linear, logical approach. In short, Paul, you are still young and so many things are getting more emphasis in our culture. You need to know that lots of doors are opening up for you. Companies are looking for people with nonconventional ideas and new ways to solve their very old problems.

The biggest thing you'll want to work on is shedding the years of frustration and disappointment that you have endured because you didn't fit the traditional mode of intelligence espoused 50 years ago. That leaves a lot of scars, but you can get past them if you allow yourself the opportunity to start over and see yourself as the truly gifted person you are. Dr. Gardner would be standing here telling you the exact same thing. Society has used models of intelligence to label and limit individuals for too long. Gardner's model is meant to empower all people, to let all of us shine and realize our full potential. I invite you to read some of his work and come to understand everything you have to offer the rest of us.

Hope this helps!

—Walter

There is still time for Paul to realize his potential and know what it is like to use his talents, because those old Industrial Age assumptions are changing quickly in society. I often think of Paul and wonder how he is doing these days. For him, MI theory means more than Gardner may have ever realized. Here is his response:

Dear Walter,

Thank you for your quick response to my inquiry. Thank you for the encouragement and information you have given me. I have no love for the educational system in my time growing up. It is my hope with this newfound gift I can help others find their potential also. Your response has given me hope and glimmer of what I can become if I apply myself with these gifts.

—Paul

For Paul, the hope of new possibilities shines in his reply. Isn't it amazing how the weight of years is lifted from his shoulders as he realizes what the future might hold for him? It seems clear that Paul was always highly aware of his abilities; he just needed to know that he could meaningfully use them to contribute to society. The messages he received as a student did not validate his strengths. In fact, his sense of purpose and worth were undermined as he struggled to fit into the prevailing definition of intelligence.

Along came Howard Gardner, who challenged that prevailing definition with one concise description of what it means to be smart: "the ability to find and solve problems and create products of value in one's own culture." It's so simple, it's profound! There is no single measurement for intelligence in this definition. There is no "quotient" that can quantify ability or predict potential. Gardner's theory attempts to provide a framework for the complex processes of human cognition without setting limits on its potential. If the human mind has an operating system, Gardner's model is the manual that attempts to explain how it runs.

21st-Century Skills

The operating system metaphor has become commonplace with the explosion of information technology over the past several decades. Students today are facing a job market built around an emerging information economy, and the "three Rs" will not sufficiently prepare students for the 21st-century workplace. While reading, writing, mathematics, and citizenship are still core components of American education, the Information Age demands that people need additional skills to remain competitive. Workers need:

Information Technology Skills. The ability to access information and manipulate it using a variety of digital tools.

Information Literacy Skills. The ability to evaluate information for validity and reliability through a variety of critical-thinking strategies.

Problem-Solving Skills. The ability to generate efficient, effective solutions that meet the needs of the marketplace.

Collaboration Skills. The ability to interact with colleagues, even in geographically disparate locations, to complete complex tasks.

Flexibility. The ability to adapt and adjust ideas as new information becomes available.

Creativity. The ability to present information and ideas in novel or unique ways in the marketplace.

Individually, each of these skills is already valued in the workplace. In combination, however, they create a profile of a worker functioning in a much more abstract environment in which goals and expectations change quickly. As we become the world's information superpower, the emphasis will be on teamwork and the marketing of ideas rather than on concrete products.

With the Information Age evolving so rapidly, how do schools adopt a new model of thinking and learning that adequately parallels society's demands? If we tend to teach in the same ways that we ourselves were taught, how then do we as teachers break away from the standardized, homogeneous approach to schooling that we knew as students? On what sound theory can those innovators in the classroom who have already recognized the changing needs of society base their evolving instructional practices?

Gardner's MI theory does an excellent job of addressing the needs of the Information Age. In fact, his intelligences nicely correspond with the very skills we have just discussed:

Information Technology Skills. The **kinesthetic** intelligence supports these skills as students manipulate tools that help them work successfully with information.

Information Literacy Skills. The **intrapersonal** and **naturalist** intelligences come into play as students identify and evaluate information for its usefulness.

Problem-Solving Skills. The **logical** intelligence operates as students offer varied ideas to solve problems.

Collaboration Skills. The **interpersonal** and **verbal** intelligences function when students interact to complete tasks and create products for the greater good.

Flexibility. The **musical** intelligence allows students to detect and follow patterns in information as it becomes available.

Creativity. The **visual** and **existential** intelligences allow students to envision ideas, solutions, and products that can improve the quality of their lives.

There has never been a better time for Gardner's ideas to take hold. They seem to answer so many questions and address so many needs in society. Perhaps this is why educators at all levels have embraced it so readily.

Effective Instruction

At the same time, technology can provide us with the tools we need to redefine how and what we teach. As the old saying goes, "If the only tool you have is a hammer, everything around you looks like a nail." There is no longer a one-size-fits-all solution for providing instruction. This is a time of great growth that can also be a time of great peril. Technology advances so quickly it's very easy to be impressed by new advancements, even to the point of letting technology take precedence over instruction. As educators, we have a responsibility to make sure that the use of technology is well grounded in sound educational theory and practice; instructional considerations must always come first. Without a sound educational foundation, instructional technology will not fulfill its promise. It will, instead, fall by the wayside like other innovations that have preceded it. In this regard we have come full circle: technology supports the accommodation of multiple intelligences in the classroom, while at the same time MI theory offers a strong theoretical foundation for the integration of technology into education (Figure 1).

FIGURE 1
The Multiple Intelligences and Instructional Technology Cycle

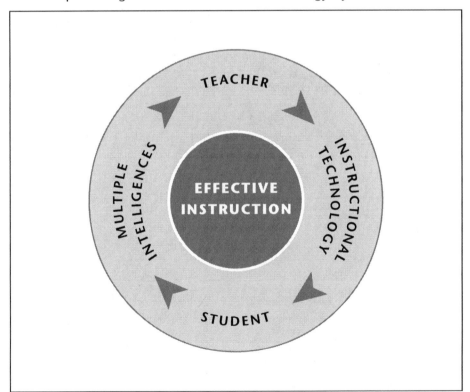

Resources Accompanying This Book

This book is meant to be a practical guide for applying Gardner's MI theory to education by integrating instructional technology into the curriculum. To make the book as useful as possible, a variety of resources and tools have been included both in the book itself and on the accompanying CD-ROM.

Among these resources are two MI surveys: one text-based survey for older students (see appendix A) and one image-based survey for students in primary grades (see appendix B).

The Multiple Intelligences Survey for Younger Students, which is a series of pictures highlighting specific activities, comes in two formats. The student version has no captions under the pictures. The Teacher Scoring Key (on the CD-ROM) includes captions identifying the target intelligences, allowing for easy interpretation of student responses.

The Multiple Intelligences Survey for Older Students also comes in two versions. The black and white version is for students, and the color-coded version is for teachers who wish to analyze survey items or break down student responses by intelligence. Both versions come in Microsoft Excel format for easy calculation and analysis. Chapter 2 explains the use of the surveys in more detail. Both surveys and both teacher scoring keys appear on the CD-ROM.

Also included in the book and on the CD-ROM are lesson, unit, and collaborative project templates for constructing MI-based instruction. A software evaluation tool and PEP (Presoftware, Experience, Postsoftware), POMAT (Procedure, Objective, Materials, Assessment, Technology), and OPP (Objective, Procedure, Product) charts for analyzing existing lessons and resources are also provided. These charts and their use are explained in detail in subsequent chapters.

It is my hope that these tools will assist you in successfully transforming your classroom into a technology-rich, intelligence-wise learning environment.

Resources for Further Study

Print

Alvermann, D. E., Moon, J. S., & Hagood, M. C. (1999). *Popular culture in the classroom: Teaching and researching critical media literacy.* Newark, DE: International Reading Association.

Csikszentmihalyi, M. (2003). *Good business: Leadership, flow, and the making of meaning.* New York: Viking Press.

Eisenberg, M. B., Lowe, C. A., & Spitzer, K. L. (2004). *Information literacy: Essential skills for the Information Age* (2nd ed.). Portsmouth, NH: Libraries Unlimited.

Gardner, H., Csikszentmihalyi, M., & Damon, W. (2002). *Good work: When excellence and ethics meet.* New York: Basic Books.

Hawisher, G., & Selfe, C. (1999). *Global literacies and the World Wide Web*. New York: Routledge.

Thornburg, D. D. (2002). *The new basics: Education and the future of work in the Telematic Age*. Alexandria, VA: Association for Supervision and Curriculum Development.

Warlick, D. (2004). *Redefining literacy for the 21st century*. Worthington, OH: Linworth.

Online

Equipped for the Future: 21st Century Skills for the New Economy:
http://eff.cls.utk.edu/PDF/eff_brochure.pdf

The Good Work Project:
www.goodworkproject.org

Integration: Building 21st Century Learning Environments:
www.landmark-project.com/edtechnot_warlick/

Job Basics in the 21st Century:
http://teacherline.pbs.org/teacherline/resources/thornburg/thornburg0401.cfm

Learning for the 21st Century:
http://21stcenturyskills.org/downloads/P21_Report.pdf

Seventeen Foundation Skills for the 21st Century:
www.careerkey.org/english/you/foundation_parents_yourchoices.html

Working in the 21st Century:
www.bls.gov/opub/working/home.htm

Reflections

1   What is the difference between viewing multiple intelligences as a theory of intelligence and as a theory of learning?

2   How does the typical classroom of today differ from the classroom of the Industrial Age?

3   In what ways do you teach the way you were taught? In what ways do you teach the way children learn?

4   In the Multiple Intelligences and Instructional Technology Cycle diagram (Figure 1), why does the teacher come between multiple intelligences and instructional technology? Why does the student come between instructional technology and multiple intelligences?

CHAPTER 2

Instructional Design and Multiple Intelligences

Since Howard Gardner first introduced his MI theory, educators have been grappling with its implications. Gardner himself does not presume to have all the answers, but rather defers to educators as the experts who can best apply his work in the classroom. To make this happen, teachers first need to know the distinguishing characteristics of each of the intelligences. This is important because it is easy to take an intelligence at face value without truly examining it for its distinct attributes and features. Too often, for example, teachers assume that the musical intelligence can be tapped merely by introducing music into a lesson, or that the naturalist intelligence can be targeted simply by studying flora and fauna in the curriculum. If we are going to effectively transform instruction by using Gardner's theory, we must understand its basic tenets. To do any less would be to compromise its usefulness as a viable model.

Intelligences Overview

Let's take a brief look at each intelligence before discussing how they can be addressed with instructional technology:

Verbal. Traditionally one of the most heavily emphasized intelligences in the classroom. It has been valued because it matches the traditional ways we have taught: lecture, recitation, textbooks, and board work. This intelligence includes the ability to express oneself orally and in writing, as well as the ability to master foreign languages.

Logical. Also highly valued in traditional instruction. This is not simply the intelligence of mathematics, but of logic and reasoning. This intelligence allows us to be problem solvers. It seeks structure in the learning environment and thrives on sequenced, orderly lessons. In the traditional classroom, students are asked to conform to the teacher's instructional approach, and this intelligence allows them to do so.

Visual. The intelligence that promotes spatial reasoning through the use of charts, graphs, maps, tables, illustrations, art, puzzles, costumes, and many other materials. More than just the ocular internalization of stimuli, visual intelligence allows students to picture ideas and solutions to problems in their minds before trying to verbalize them or put them into practice.

Kinesthetic. The intelligence stimulated by active, physical interaction with one's environment. The kinesthetic intelligence is promoted through fine and gross motor activities, such as those found in manipulative learning centers, science labs, active games, and dramatic improvisations. Students with a strong kinesthetic intelligence may seem "overactive" in the traditional classroom, but they thrive in hands-on learning environments.

Musical. The intelligence of patterns, including songs, poetry, instruments, environmental sounds, and rhythms. By picking up the patterns in different situations, learners are able to make sense of their environment and adapt successfully. Note that this is not exclusively an auditory intelligence; it can include all kinds of patterns. Because mathematics is defined as the study of patterns, this is truly the domain of mathematics instruction.

Intrapersonal. The intelligence of feelings, values, and attitudes. This intelligence helps the learner make an affective connection with the curriculum. Children who ask, "Why do I need to learn this?" or "How does this affect me?" are exercising their intrapersonal intelligence. It is the part of us that expects learning to be meaningful. The more we find pertinence in what we study, the more inclined we are to take ownership for our learning and the better we will retain what we have learned.

Interpersonal. The intelligence stimulated by interactions with others. Students who are strong in this intelligence often require collaboration to make sense of learning. Students with a strong interpersonal tendency may have been labeled "too talkative" or "excessively social" in the traditional classroom. Properly guided, these students thrive in cooperative groups, in partnerships, or even in whole-group settings where they are free to ask, discuss, and understand.

Naturalist. The intelligence of categories and hierarchies. While the naturalist intelligence does include the study of plants, animals, and other sciences, consider the processes that these disciplines promote and require: classification, categorization, and hierarchical frameworks. The naturalist intelligence can be stimulated in the classroom through activities such as attribute grouping, charting, and semantic mapping.

Existential. The intelligence of understanding processes within a larger, existential context. It can include aesthetics, philosophy, and religion and emphasizes the classical values of beauty, truth, and goodness. This intelligence allows students to see their place in the big picture, whether that is the classroom, the community, the world, or the universe. Students with a strong existential intelligence have the ability to summarize and synthesize ideas from many disciplines and sources. While Gardner is still not satisfied that he has enough physiological evidence to conclusively establish this as an intelligence, I am including it here for the purposes of our discussion. After all, who has not observed this intelligence in the classroom?

Now, consider how we have traditionally classified and taught academic disciplines, and how these disciplines line up with the intelligences (Figure 2).

FIGURE 2
Traditional Classification of Disciplines and Multiple Intelligences

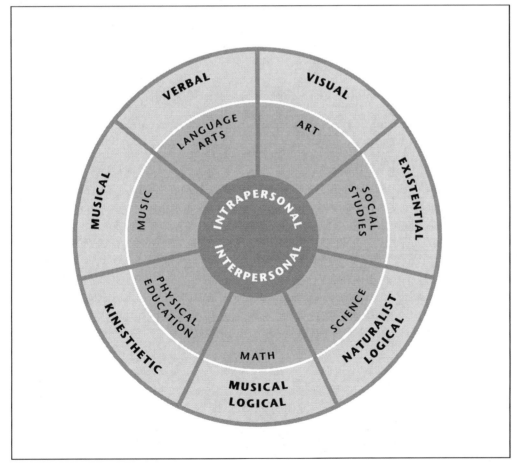

In Figure 2, notice how much one-to-one correspondence there is between subject areas and intelligences! This reflects the schematic nature of education in the Industrial Age: each academic area receives specific attention through a quantifiable amount of time in the school day. Reading instruction takes place in its own distinct time block, and has nothing to do with what goes on during math instruction. Addressing each discipline within its own time slot is assumed to be an efficient, practical approach to education.

Note, too, how the musical intelligence is distributed across both music and mathematics instruction. Given everything coming out of brain research over the past 20 years about the connection between exposure to music and success in mathematics, this makes an enormous amount of sense. Both disciplines concern themselves with the study of patterns.

Notice especially the void when it comes to the intra- and interpersonal intelligences. Where is time allotted for these paths to learning in the traditional school day? From a traditional instructional point of view, there is no place in the school day for affective or social learning. The goal of Industrial Age education is standardization: one size fits all. The goal is not to promote individual differences but to create an educated citizenry that possesses a common set of skills. Do students sometimes get the opportunity to interact or share their feelings and attitudes? Of course, but that is not a traditional goal of instruction. If you need to express your feelings, you speak to the teacher outside of class, or visit the nurse or guidance counselor. If you are inclined to talk and interact with your classmates, lunch and recess times are your prime opportunities to do so. After all, a quiet classroom is a productive classroom!

The way we have traditionally looked at instruction—by subject area—may well hamper our ability to look at intelligences holistically across the curriculum. Addressing a student's verbal intelligence solely through a language arts time slot is convenient and comfortable. But today, all the intelligences need to be engaged across the curriculum. Students should be using their verbal intelligence in math just as they should be using their logical intelligence in the arts. The kinesthetic intelligence must be actuated in the science classroom just as the visual intelligence must be stimulated in social studies. And the interpersonal and intrapersonal intelligences (which Gardner equates with Goldman's emotional intelligence) must also be accommodated in all areas of instruction.

Consider the observable actions for each intelligence shown in Table 1.

TABLE 1

Multiple Intelligences Observable Actions

INTELLIGENCE	OBSERVABLE ACTIONS
Verbal	Read, write, speak, tell, ask, explain, inform, convey, report, articulate, address, confer, request, recount, lecture, present, announce, narrate, debate, discuss, converse, recite, quote, describe, clarify
Logical	Solve, resolve, question, hypothesize, theorize, scrutinize, investigate, experiment, analyze, deduce, prove, verify, decipher, determine, predict, estimate, measure, calculate, quantify, simplify
Visual	Observe, symbolize, draw, sketch, draft, illustrate, paint, color, contour, outline, rearrange, design, redesign, invent, create, conceive, originate, innovate, imagine, picture, envision, visualize, pretend
Kinesthetic	Build, construct, erect, assemble, make, manufacture, structure, craft, imitate, play, perform, walk, run, jump, dance, collect, gather, compile, fashion, shape, duplicate, dissect, exercise, move, transport
Musical	Listen, hear, infer, audit, note, pattern, sing, clap, chant, model, repeat, replicate, reproduce, copy, echo, imitate, impersonate, mimic, compose, harmonize, dub, rap, orchestrate, resonate
Intrapersonal	Express, imply, support, sponsor, promote, advise, advocate, encourage, champion, justify, rationalize, characterize, defend, validate, vindicate, assess, evaluate, judge, challenge, survey, poll
Interpersonal	Share, lead, guide, direct, help, mediate, manage, conduct, collaborate, cooperate, interview, influence, persuade, campaign, convince, compromise, role-play, improvise, ad-lib, referee, reconcile
Naturalist	Sort, organize, categorize, compare, contrast, differentiate, separate, classify, detail, align, order, arrange, sequence, inventory, catalogue, group, file, index, chronicle, log, map, chart, graph
Existential	Reflect, contemplate, deliberate, ponder, summarize, synthesize, associate, relate, recap, encapsulate, elaborate, appreciate, appraise, critique, evaluate, assess, speculate, explore, dream, wonder

Notice how these verbs suggest specific processes that help to clarify the functions of each intelligence, while at the same time suggesting areas of overlap. It is crucial that we understand that everyone possesses all these intelligences; they act in concert and are not mutually exclusive. Therefore, it is incorrect to label a child as a "kinesthetic learner" or a "verbal learner." This is the tendency of the learning styles model, which is not consistent with MI theory. Our goal should be to provide instructional opportunities that promote all nine intelligences. MI theory was not developed to label or exclude individuals, but to promote success for all learners by allowing them to choose different paths to learning. So, while the intelligences function as distinct entities, there is also a great deal of overlap as we observe them operating in the classroom. We can break the intelligences down into distinct domains to study their unique characteristics, but it is important to bring them back together into one holistic model when we begin to discuss their role in instruction.

Multiple Intelligences Survey

To appreciate the distribution of intelligences in your classroom, it may be helpful to administer an MI survey to your students. The following survey is not a test but an inventory of learner preferences. It is not offered as a definitive measurement of a static intelligence, but as a snapshot of how your students currently perceive their strengths in all nine intelligences. This survey should not be used to label or categorize students. It is simply an opportunity for you to appreciate the unique distribution of intelligences within each of your students, and across your classroom.

The survey is available in Microsoft Excel spreadsheet format on the accompanying CD-ROM. Students can enter the data on the inventory sheet by typing a "1" if they agree with the statement or a "0" if they disagree. As a subject enters his or her responses, Excel automatically calculates the MI profile on a second tab of the survey. Table 2 shows a sample completed survey.

TABLE 2

A Completed Multiple Intelligences Survey for Older Students

For each statement, enter a number one (1) if you agree with the statement or enjoy the activity being described. Enter a number zero (0) if you do not.

I LIKE...		I LIKE...	
Sorting things into groups.	1	Chatting online.	0
Thinking about life.	1	Having strong feelings about things.	1
Picturing things in my mind.	0	Playing sports.	1
Working with my hands.	1	Studying religion.	0
Studying patterns.	0	Making art.	0
Keeping things in order.	1	Moving to a beat.	0
Studying with a partner.	1	Writing stories.	1
Looking at the big picture.	0	Solving problems.	0
Learning a new language.	0	Completing a word-find puzzle.	0
Being right.	1	Being on a team.	1
Listening to sounds in nature.	1	Drawing maps.	1
Moving around.	0	Hiking and camping.	0
Making up nonsense words.	0	Playing an instrument.	0
Following directions.	1	Practicing sign language.	1
Protecting nature.	0	Studying art.	1
Decorating a room.	1	Having things neat and tidy.	0

(Continued)

A Completed Multiple Intelligences Survey for Older Students

(Continued)

I LIKE...		I LIKE...	
Studying different countries.	0	Working alone.	1
Being fair.	1	Observing the stars and planets.	0
Writing in a diary.	0	Using my imagination.	1
Rhyming words.	0	Learning about animals.	0
Watching a play.	0	Listening to all kinds of music.	0
Working in a garden.	0	Using tools.	0
Figuring out math problems.	0	Joining a club.	1
Being a good friend.	1	Discussing world issues.	1
Listening to music.	0	Being a leader.	1
Talking on the phone.	1	Giving a speech.	1
Wondering about the universe.	0	Marching to a beat.	0
Exercising.	1	Knowing why I should do something.	1
Visiting national parks.	0	Keeping things neat.	0
Feeling good about my work.	0	Summarizing ideas.	1
Remembering poems or words to songs.	0	Building things.	0
Creating graphs and charts.	1	Recycling waste.	1
Making timelines.	0	Taking notes.	1
Having a debate.	1	Working with others.	0
Getting along with others.	0	Planning things in my mind.	0
Putting together a puzzle.	0	Wondering about life on other planets.	1
Reading charts and tables.	0	Being treated fairly.	0
Making arts and crafts.	1	Going to the zoo.	1
Helping the poor.	0	Making lists.	1
Being with other people.	1	Playing charades.	1
Answering riddles.	1	Listening to a story.	0
Watching a video.	0	Reading books.	1
Writing letters.	1	Being around other people.	1
Dancing.	0	Spending time outdoors.	1
Having background noise while I work.	1	Sensing something is about to happen.	1
Speaking up when I see something wrong.	1		

Once the survey is completed, students can click on the corresponding Scoring sheet tab to see their MI profile (Figure 3). By highlighting the range of cells and selecting the Chart Wizard button, they can see a graphic representation of their profile. Be sure to discuss with your class how these results can help them appreciate all the ways they can learn!

FIGURE 3

Sample of MI Survey Scoring Report

Multiple Intelligences Survey Scoring Report

To graph your results, simply highlight the range B6:C22 and click on the Chart Wizard Button.

				Percentage out of 30 items		Proportion out of 100%
Verbal	6		Analytic	50%		31%
Logical	4		Interactive	53%		33%
Visual	6		Introspective	57%		35%
						out of
Musical	6					100%
Kinesthetic	3					
Interpersonal	7		Strongest Domain	57%		
Intrapersonal	7					
Naturalist	5					
Existential	4					

The accompanying CD-ROM also includes a primary inventory for nonreaders. Students are asked to choose from a set of 27 pictures, circling each image that represents an activity they like to do. Figure 4 shows a sample of this survey. Once the survey has been completed, the teacher can do a quick tally of intelligence preferences using the separate key. Some children may be inclined to circle most of or all the pictures in the survey. For these students, simply change the directions and ask them to place an X over each image they do not like to do. This will place the student in a more critical mind-set that will give you a better idea of his or her true preferences.

FIGURE 4

Sample From Multiple Intelligences Survey for Younger Students

MULTIPLE INTELLIGENCES SURVEY FOR YOUNGER STUDENTS

STUDENT NAME _____

Circle each picture that shows an activity you like to do.

Remember:

- Everyone has all the intelligences.

- You can strengthen an intelligence.

- These inventories are meant as a snapshot in time. Intelligence preferences can change.

- MI theory is meant to empower people, not label them.

Are there more intelligences? There certainly may well be. Gardner prefers to work with a manageable group of broad categories rather than dozens and dozens of narrowly defined intelligences. In the case of the existential intelligence, for example, he originally catalogued a number of possible attributes for a "spiritualist" intelligence until he realized that, if he backed up and looked at more general traits, there might be a way to combine them into a more identifiable and measurable category.

What other intelligences may yet be discovered? Gardner concedes he does not know, but he suggests that teachers may be a great source for future research in this area. After all, education is the one profession that dedicates its expertise to observing human learning and then diagnosing and prescribing instruction. What do you think might be a viable candidate as the next intelligence?

Relationships Among the Intelligences

Having these basic definitions of each intelligence in place is important, but not as important as having a working understanding of how the intelligences relate to one another. After all, if these different paths to learning always act in concert, we're not going to be able to take full advantage of this model unless we look at all the intelligences in operation together. This can be difficult to do, because once you begin observing a specific child the intelligences become very fluid and free flowing. What might be easily recognizable in isolation becomes much less clear when observing holistically.

For example, let's say that Chris is building a working 6-inch by 2-inch car model using her knowledge of simple machines. She's working with two classmates at a learning center her teacher has prepared. Together they have made a wooden chassis and placed wheels and axles on its four points. This morning they are conducting practice runs of their car down an inclined plane, testing to see how adding weight to the chassis can improve the car's performance. The critical question they are asking themselves is, "Where is the best place to add weight to the car to maximize its speed moving down an inclined plane?"

As an observer, which intelligences do you see Chris using? Certainly the kinesthetic and interpersonal intelligences are evident. How about running the trials and recording the car speed based on the placement of weight. Is that more of a logical activity? Since they're looking for patterns based on repeated trials, would this be a rhythmic task? And if they're creating a table that organizes their data so that they can make sense of their findings, wouldn't that employ the naturalist intelligence? Intelligences are not so clear-cut once you begin observing learners in their environment.

To further illustrate the point, consider Sandy Hare's first-grade simple machines unit (Table 3).

TABLE 3

Simple Machines Lesson

LESSON TITLE: Simple Machines, Forces, Motion, and Friction
TEACHER: Sandy Hare, Wells Elementary School, Tehachapi, California
GRADE LEVEL: 1
SUBJECT(S): Physical Science   **TIME FRAME:** 5 days

OBJECTIVE(S)	INTELLIGENCES	TECHNOLOGIES	STANDARDS
• Students will identify and describe at least five kinds of simple machines.	Verbal Kinesthetic	Manipulative science centers	**NETS for Students:** **3. Technology productivity tools** • Students use technology tools to enhance learning, increase productivity, and promote creativity.
• Students will identify several forces or types of energy that simple machines use to make work easier.	Logical Kinesthetic	Computer science center	
• Students will understand that living organisms produce energy from sunlight or from other organisms, but that simple machines must be supplied with energy by people.	Logical Kinesthetic Intrapersonal Existential	Leprechaun Trap homework and instructions worksheets	• Students use productivity tools to collaborate in constructing technology-enhanced models, preparing publications, and producing other creative works.
• Students will identify several kinds of motion used by simple machines.	Logical Kinesthetic		**5. Technology research tools** • Students use technology to locate, evaluate, and collect information from a variety of sources.
• Students will be able to predict where an object will move when a force is used to change its direction.	Logical Naturalist Musical Interpersonal		**6. Technology problem-solving and decision-making tools** • Students use technology resources for solving problems and making informed decisions.
• Students will be able to measure and compare the distances an object rolls on smooth and rough surfaces.	Logical Kinesthetic Visual		
• Students will understand that friction can slow down an object's motion.	Logical Kinesthetic		• Students employ technology in the development of strategies for solving problems in the real world.

(Continued)

Simple Machines Lesson

(Continued)

MATERIALS	INTELLIGENCES
Hardware Internet-ready computer, scan converter, TV monitor, printer, VCR, digital camera, overhead projector, screen	Verbal Logical Visual
Software Learn About Physical Science: Simple Machines (Sunburst) Kidspiration (Inspiration Software) Kid Pix (Broderbund) EasyBook (Sunburst) or online software program Create a Shape Book (ABC Teach) (www.abcteach.com)	Musical Kinesthetic Interpersonal Intrapersonal Naturalist Existential Visual
Web Sites www.brainpop.com/tech/seeall.weml BrainPop! has two simple machine movies: *Inclined Planes* and *Levers*.	Visual Logical
www.edheads.org/activities/simple-machines/ Edheads Web site has animations of six simple machines, with an interactive quiz on each. Excellent graphics, too!	Visual Logical
www.smartown.com/sp2000/machines2000/smallframe.htm Smartown Web site has music, more difficult, but eye-catching explanations, and photographs of elementary school students and their machines.	Visual Logical
www.funderstanding.com/k12/coaster/ Funderstanding Roller Coaster lets kids design a coaster by manipulating mass, gravity, slope, friction, and speed.	Verbal
Manipulatives Marble chutes set, marble towers set, Gears! set, make-it-yourself set (building blocks, toy cars, clay), Rollero creativity station	Kinesthetic Logical
Computer Science Center BrainPop! Web site movies: *Levers, Inclined Planes* Learning About Physical Science: Simple Machines software Edheads Web site Smartown's Small Frame Web site	Verbal Visual Logical Kinesthetic
Other Materials *Simple Machines* minibook *Harcourt Brace Science Big Book, Extension Unit* Harcourt Brace science video HB Science practice, assessment, and project worksheets drawing and writing paper Leprechaun Trap homework and worksheets crayons, markers, paint (preferably acrylic), toilet paper/paper towel tubes, wood or plastic building blocks, cardboard and wood scraps (for ramps)	Visual Verbal Verbal Logical Kinesthetic

PROCEDURE

Preparation Two weeks before St. Patrick's Day, talk about how tricky, contrary, and greedy for gold leprechauns are. Perhaps visit a Web site with pictures and information about leprechauns.	Verbal Intrapersonal Existential

(Continued)

Simple Machines Lesson

(Continued)

PROCEDURE	INTELLIGENCES
Assign "Build Your Own Leprechaun Trap" homework. Brainstorm ideas for trapping leprechauns.	Verbal Visual
When traps are returned on St. Patrick's Day, have students write instructions that explain how each leprechaun trap works. Have students display their traps on their desks. Invite other classes to the classroom to admire the traps. Have each trap creator explain and demonstrate how his or her leprechaun trap works.	Verbal Visual Interpersonal
At the end of the day, ask the class, "Did you know that you have just built a simple machine?" Demonstrate how a trap door, a bucket on a string, or a wedge work together to trap a sneaky leprechaun!	Logical Naturalist
Activities **Day 1** Read and discuss *HB Science Big Book, Extension Unit,* chapter 1, lesson 1 (What Makes Things Move?) and lesson 2 (What Are Some Ways Things Move?). Watch the companion HB video. Display lesson 2 (Force) of Simple Machines CD. Demonstrate gravity using a ramp. Do the HB "Push" activity with pencils, craft sticks, and classroom objects. Set out and explain three science centers: the marble chutes set, the marble towers set, and Sunburst's Simple Machines software. Complete any HB practice worksheets, then have students go to the centers. Play the BrainPop! movie *Inclined Planes.*	Verbal Visual Logical Kinesthetic
Day 2 Read and discuss *HB Science Big Book, Extension Unit,* chapter 1, lesson 3 (Why Do Things Move the Way They Do?). Do the HB motion activity with ramps, toy cars, and hand-made "stops" (perhaps made of clay). Demonstrate spinning and back-and-forth motions with a top, a Slinky, a paddle ball, and gears. Set out and explain Gears! manipulatives at a fourth science center. Hand out *Simple Machines* minibook. Read and discuss, find different types of motion for each machine, and go on a treasure hunt for simple machines in the classroom. Play the BrainPop! movie *Levers.* Finish with a rotation at two of the four centers.	Verbal Visual Logical Kinesthetic Interpersonal Naturalist
Day 3 Read and discuss HB Science Big Book, Extension Unit, chapter 1, lesson 4 (How Do Objects Move On Surfaces?). Identify the different combinations of motions and force. Demonstrate how an object (a toy car or marble) changes direction (is deflected or stopped) when a force (a clay barrier, bump, or rough surface) is applied. Complete any relevant HB practice worksheet. Add the Edhead Web site to the computer science center and explain it. Add a "make-it-yourself" center (with inclined planes, clay bumps, and toy cars). Do two more center rotations.	Verbal Visual Logical Kinesthetic Interpersonal Intrapersonal Naturalist
Day 4 Review the six types of simple machines studied so far. Read *HB Science Big Book, Extension Unit,* chapter 1, lesson 5 (How Do Wheels Help Things Move?). Ask the class about the differences between the ways living things produce and use energy and motion, and the ways simple machines get and use energy and motion. Hold a Rollero Race Day in which decorated toilet paper tubes are rolled down a smooth ramp. Have the fastest and farthest rolling Rollero creators each organize a team of experts. Each team will be responsible for designing and creating six different Rolleroes: (1) fastest to reach a certain point beyond the ramp, (2) farthest/straightest-rolling, (3) slowest to reach the bottom of the ramp, (4) shortest distance rolled, (5) best-decorated "Monster Rollero," and (6) best "Crazy Wheels" Rollero.	Verbal Visual Logical Kinesthetic Interpersonal Intrapersonal Naturalist Existential

(Continued)

Simple Machines Lesson

(Continued)

PROCEDURE	INTELLIGENCES
Day 5 and Beyond Add a Rollero creativity station to the above-mentioned centers. Assign each Rollero team one rotation through each center. Allow each team enough time at the Rollero creativity station to design, decorate, and test their Rolleroes. In addition, assign each team the task of designing and making two inclined planes out of cardboard, blocks, sandpaper, and other items as you see fit. Assign each child, or pairs of children, the job of finishing all nine tasks of the Simple Machines software. Assign each child the job of completing the tasks at the Edhead Simple Machine Web site during their computer lab. Add Smartown's Small Frame Web site to the computer center. Add the Funderstanding Roller Coaster Web site to the computer science center so that students can visualize and experiment with speed, slope, friction, and so on, after they finish the Edhead quizzes. Administer written assessments as time permits. Teach and have students practice the "Push-Pull Song" on the Simple Machines software. Allow enough time for each team to experience all five manipulative science centers again: marble chutes set, marble towers set, Gears! set, make-it-yourself set, and Rollero creativity station. Also, allow the children to revisit the computer science center.	Verbal Visual Logical Musical Kinesthetic Interpersonal Intrapersonal Naturalist Existential
PRODUCT	
Build-a-machine homework project	Verbal Visual Logical Kinesthetic Interpersonal Intrapersonal Naturalist Existential
ASSESSMENT	
Checklist for build-a-machine homework project: ☐ Student builds something that has the elements of a simple machine. ☐ The simple machine serves a purpose (works or moves). ☐ Student can identify the kind of simple machine built. ☐ Student describes (in verbal or written form) how the simple machine works. ☐ *Bonus:* Student's project is a complex machine (consists of more than one simple machine part).	Verbal Visual Logical Kinesthetic Interpersonal Intrapersonal Naturalist Existential

What intelligences come into play in Sandy's unit? Are certain intelligences emphasized more than others? Are certain intelligences targeted because they are best suited for first graders? Are all of the intelligences accommodated? Should they be?

When I present Gardner's theory to educators, they always come up with questions about this overlapping of intelligences. We are so accustomed to theories that package teaching and learning into neat little compartments that we tend to cling to the individual integrity of each intelligence. It's hard to let go and accept the fact that, since Gardner's theory is based on the way these intelligences actually function in human cognition, it's less easy to compartmentalize things into tidy packages. Once teachers get past the traditional definition of intelligence and our tendency to assign an intelligence to a compartmentalized subject area, there are powerful new possibilities for learning in the classroom.

The Wheel of MI Domains

Use the Wheel of MI Domains (Figure 5) to visualize the fluid relationship among the different intelligences. First, the intelligences are grouped into three regions, or domains: the interactive, analytic, and introspective. These three domains are meant to align the intelligences with familiar learner attributes teachers routinely observe in the classroom.

FIGURE 5
Wheel of MI Domains

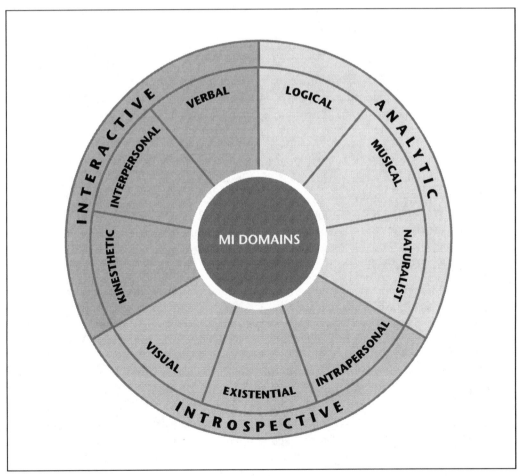

The Interactive Domain

The interactive domain consists of the verbal, interpersonal, and kinesthetic intelligences. Learners typically employ these intelligences to express themselves and explore their environment.

Consider 5-year-old Dan in his kindergarten classroom. He not only uses language to demonstrate his knowledge or express his needs, he also uses it to explore, inquire, and prompt responses from others. This can include using nonsensical expressions, repetitive recounting of favorite books, and even reverting to "baby talk." Regardless of the many language functions Dan is using, he consistently uses talk to interact with others and his environment.

Eleven-year-old Miranda provides a prime example of the interactive function of interpersonal intelligence. As her class reads E. G. Speare's *The Witch of Blackbird Pond*, she continually asks her teacher about the mores of 17th-century New England. Miranda initiates class discussion on the social dynamics of prosecuting witches in Colonial New England, not for the sake of the discussion itself, but to help her better understand the plot and setting of the story. When it comes time to be assessed for comprehension of the novel, Miranda excels in an interview format, in which she can discuss her understandings and ideas at length. In fact, her teacher offers several assessment options, including the opportunity to be interviewed by a classmate as the heroine from the book.

Finally, consider Lin's use of her kinesthetic intelligence as an interactive process. Lin has been learning about electrical circuits in her third-grade class. This week the teacher has set up an experiment at a learning center, where Lin and her classmates must use batteries, copper wiring, and light bulbs to create electrical circuits. Lin and her group of three classmates quickly create a complete circuit. They then ask their teacher for some paper clips so they can experiment making a switch that will open and close the circuit. Finally Lin's group takes the experiment a step further by creating a parallel circuit using two light bulbs. Lin has repeatedly interacted with her environment and her peers to create a greater understanding of electrical circuits.

I characterize each of these three intelligences as interactive because even though they can be stimulated through passive activity, they typically invite and encourage interaction to achieve understanding. Even if students complete a task individually, they must consider others through the way they write, create, construct, and arrive at conclusions. The interactive intelligences are by nature social processes.

The Analytic Domain

The analytic domain consists of the musical, logical, and naturalist intelligences, which promote the learner's analysis of data and knowledge.

Consider Ms. Melinski's class. Her students have created instruments that simulate the sounds of the rainforest, and the children are now using these sounds to create their own individual compositions. As the children come before the class to present and conduct their compositions, they must follow the patterns of sound and imitate them accurately to successfully perform the piece. There is a careful auditory analysis of each rhythm presented to the class, and in cases where the student has created sheet music with symbols for playing the different instruments, there is a visual analysis of patterns as well.

The logical intelligence has a highly analytical component. Consider Uri and Celeste, who are creating a bridge out of Popsicle sticks that will be able to hold the weight of a motorized 12-pound truck as it crosses the structure. They have studied many kinds of bridges and are applying their learning to make a structure strong enough to successfully do the job. As they attempt different designs, they are careful to analyze their failures and build on their successes. After two weeks of working a little every day, Uri and Celeste come up with a design that effectively and safely supports the truck's weight. Problem solving is a very analytical process!

Finally, consider Suzanne, who is asked to sort leaves by different attributes at a first-grade learning center. She sorts them by color, then by size, then by texture. As she comes up with a leaf classification system that makes sense to her, she glues each leaf to a large sheet of paper that serves as an organizer. She then displays her leaf classification system in the classroom so that the children can compare and contrast each other's strategies for classification.

I characterize these three intelligences as analytic because even though they can have a social or introspective component, they most fundamentally promote the analysis and incorporation of data into existing schema. The analytical intelligences are by nature heuristic processes.

The Introspective Domain

The introspective domain consists of the existential, intrapersonal, and visual intelligences. These intelligences have a distinctly affective component. In the case of visual intelligence, consider Michelangelo celebrating the discovery of a large slab of marble because he wants to free the angel he sees within it through his act of sculpting. There is a uniquely emotional component to visualizing a piece of art before actually creating it. In the same way, recall a student you have worked with who served as a class leader simply because he or she was able to visualize where to go with a project before the rest of the group was even prepared to begin discussing the possibilities. There is an intuitive release of energy that sparks the enthusiasm and imagination of others when the visual intelligence is unleashed.

The existential intelligence displays similar emotional, introspective characteristics. When Soeren Kierkegaard described looking at the infinite depth of the night sky and having an emotionally charged response that said, "Yes, I am part of something bigger in the universe!" he was referring to this experience. It is necessary to make that leap of faith in order to contribute to the collective human experience. This can also be experienced in the presence of great works of art, such as the Pieta. As the senses take in the aesthetic beauty of one of humankind's great expressions of human love and suffering, the emotional release moves many unsuspecting onlookers to tears.

The intrapersonal intelligence may be the most obvious example of this. Consider 14-year-old Kristin, who filters everything she learns through her strong sense of social justice. She lights up when learning about the plight of Native Americans in the 19th century, the ethical dilemmas posed by genetic engineering, and the tragedy of apartheid in Alan Paton's *Cry, the Beloved Country*. Kristin volunteers at her local party headquarters and campaigns for the local and national political candidates of her choice. Everything Kristin learns is reinforced and mastered by the emotional connection she has with the material she is studying.

I characterize these three intelligences as introspective because they require a looking inward by the learner, an emotive connection to their own experiences and beliefs in order to make sense of new learning. The introspective intelligences are by nature affective processes.

Using the Wheel of MI Domains

By using the Wheel of MI Domains, we can begin to get a handle on the interaction of the various intelligences in the classroom. These domains, like the intelligences themselves, are not discrete, separable entities. Just as bridge building can be seen as a strongly logical activity, it also requires interpersonal, verbal, kinesthetic, visual, and even musical and naturalist components. The wheel reminds us to seek a balance when planning activities and instruction so that all the intelligences are brought together at a central point.

When planning an MI-based lesson, consider using the wheel to select one intelligence from each domain. This will help you create a well-rounded lesson that stimulates a broad range of intelligences. For example, Joseph's lesson on soliloquies may benefit from using the verbal (interactive), musical (analytic), and existential (introspective) intelligences. By tapping into all three ways of knowing, he accommodates learning in different ways. The lesson might look like this:

Objective

Given a soliloquy selected from *Macbeth*, the learner will recite the soliloquy with proper meter and correctly interpret its content.

Intelligences

Verbal. Reciting the soliloquy
Musical. Understanding the soliloquy's meter
Existential. Interpreting the sentiment expressed in the soliloquy

Then again, a teacher may decide to target one domain in a lesson and select two or three intelligences from the same domain to emphasize their interconnection. When dissecting earthworms, for example, Peter wants to emphasize the analytical nature of the task. He decides to map the logical, musical, and naturalist intelligences in this lesson:

Objective

Given an earthworm to dissect, the learner will follow specific step-by-step instructions, categorizing organs by body systems and identifying patterns found within those systems.

Intelligences

Logical. Following sequential directions
Musical. Identifying patterns within the body structure
Naturalist. Categorizing organs by body system

The Wheel of MI Domains can be a helpful tool in creating lessons that are balanced, targeted, and responsive to the distribution of intelligences in your classroom.

Resources for Further Study

Print

Armstrong, T. (2000). *Multiple intelligences in the classroom* (2nd ed.). Alexandria, VA: Association for Supervision and Curriculum Development.

Campbell, L., Campbell, B., & Dickinson, D. (2003). *Teaching and learning through multiple intelligences* (3rd ed.). Upper Saddle River, NJ: Allyn & Bacon.

Carreiro, P. (1998). *Tales of thinking: Multiple intelligences in the classroom.* Columbus, OH: Stenhouse.

Gardner, H. (1983). *Frames of mind: The theory of multiple intelligences.* New York: Basic Books.

Gardner, H. (2000). *Intelligence reframed: Multiple intelligences for the 21st century.* New York: Basic Books.

Hoerr, T. R. (2000). *Becoming a multiple intelligences school.* Alexandria, VA: Association for Supervision and Curriculum Development.

Nardi, D. (2001). *Multiple intelligences and personality type: Tools and strategies for developing human potential.* Huntington Beach, CA: Telos.

Online

Extra! Extra! Interview With Howard Gardner:
www.nea.org/neatoday/9903/gardner.html

Multiple Intelligences Immersion:
http://surfaquarium.com/MI/intelligences.htm

Multiple Intelligences Overview:
http://surfaquarium.com/MI/overview.htm

On Teaching for Understanding: A Conversation With Howard Gardner:
www.ascd.org/publications/ed_lead/199304/brandt.html

Tapping Into Multiple Intelligences:
www.thirteen.org/edonline/concept2class/month1/

Teachers Should Diversify Approaches to Teaching, Gardner Says:
www.weac.org/aboutwea/conven97/gardner2.htm

The Theory of Multiple Intelligences:
www.edwebproject.org/edref.mi.intro.html

Reflections

1 Review your state standards and determine whether they target the intelligences in compartmentalized subject areas or across the curriculum. How can you implement these standards utilizing all the intelligences?

2 How are the different intelligences distributed in your classroom based on the MI survey? Which were the top three intelligence scores for your class? Which were the bottom three scores?

3 How can the information you gathered from the MI survey be used in future instruction?

4 When is it most appropriate to develop lesson plans that target the same domain on the MI wheel? When is it most appropriate to plan using intelligences from different domains? Why?

CHAPTER 3

Technology and Multiple Intelligences

Over the years, technology has flooded the field of education with many promises made on many dollars spent. Teachers have done their best to ride the recurrent waves of new hardware, software, and best practices, each one better than the last, all implicitly promising to revolutionize teaching and learning. Ask teachers about their experience with technology, and they will tell you of victories and struggles, good intentions and naive assumptions, promising hits and dispiriting misses. Now that we are being asked to account for all that spending and the effect it has had on learning, it seems painfully obvious that we have to rethink our priorities as far as educational technology is concerned. Education needs leaders who will help set those priorities.

Crafting Technology Standards

The International Society for Technology in Education (ISTE) has developed a set of six National Educational Technology Standards for Students (NETS•S) to help teachers harness the power of technology in their instructional planning. The standards were developed not only to promote learning through the effective use of technology, but to foster those high-tech job skills that will be in such demand in the years to come.

There are six broad standards with descriptive performance indicators for each. The standards are written to help us prioritize our implementation of instructional technology. Note how ISTE's standards match up with Gardner's intelligences when considering appropriate student uses of technology.

A Comparison of ISTE's NETS for Students and Gardner's Intelligences

1 Basic operations and concepts

- Students demonstrate a sound understanding of the nature and operation of technology systems.

   Logical, naturalist. Explain the organization of different systems and how they function.

- Students are proficient in the use of technology.

   Kinesthetic. Manipulate digital and industrial technologies for goal-oriented tasks.

2 Social, ethical, and human issues

- Students understand the ethical, cultural, and societal issues related to technology.

   Intrapersonal, existential. Understand and internalize the individual and communal values that govern technology use.

- Students practice responsible use of technology systems, information, and software.

   Intrapersonal, existential. Internalize and practice the individual and communal values that govern technology use.

- Students develop positive attitudes toward technology uses that support lifelong learning, collaboration, personal pursuits, and productivity.

   Intrapersonal, existential. Develop attitudes that will promote technology use to improve quality of life.

3 Technology productivity tools

- Students use technology tools to enhance learning, increase productivity, and promote creativity.

   Verbal, kinesthetic, visual. Use technology to apply knowledge in new and different ways.

- Students use productivity tools to collaborate in constructing technology-enhanced models, preparing publications, and producing other creative works.

  Verbal, kinesthetic, interpersonal, visual. Participate in groups that apply technology tools to enhance learning.

4 Technology communications tools

- Students use telecommunications to collaborate, publish, and interact with peers, experts, and other audiences.

  Verbal, interpersonal. Virtually interact with one another in completing goal-oriented tasks.

- Students use a variety of media and formats to communicate information and ideas effectively to multiple audiences.

  Verbal, musical, interpersonal. Use the various features and properties of technology to demonstrate learning to others.

5 Technology research tools

- Students use technology to locate, evaluate, and collect information from a variety of sources.

  Verbal, logical, naturalist, intrapersonal. Access, categorize, and evaluate information for specific tasks.

- Students use technology tools to process data and report results.

  Verbal, logical, musical, naturalist. Format research results into clean, organized, well-developed presentations.

- Students evaluate and select new information resources and technological innovations based on the appropriateness to specific tasks.

  Intrapersonal, naturalist. Analyze data and technologies within the context of an assigned task to determine their value.

6 Technology problem-solving and decision-making tools

- Students use technology resources for solving problems and making informed decisions.

  Logical, intrapersonal, existential. Use technology to make appropriate choices based on the data provided.

- Students employ technology in the development of strategies for solving problems in the real world.

  Logical, intrapersonal, existential. Use technology to generate effective solutions to problems that can improve the quality of life.

The ISTE NETS for Students address all of Gardner's intelligences in broad, well-rounded categories. By using these standards as guidelines for planning technology use in your classroom, building, and district, you can help ensure that instruction accommodates the whole range of intelligences and technologies. With the standards as a firm foundation on which we can build, let's take a closer look at the different kinds of technologies available in the classroom.

Industrial Technologies

What comes to mind when you think of technology? If you were born before the last quarter of the 20th century, the word will likely conjure images of construction sites, factories, and farm machinery. These were familiar sights long before the advent of computers. Industrial technologies have revolutionized our ability to do work, to use machines and engines to create goods and provide services more efficiently and economically. They have transformed the world from an agrarian economy to an industrial marketplace, bringing nations and cultures closer over time. Still, Industrial Age tools largely depend on the skills and expertise of the humans who wield them. Roles become more specialized on an assembly line, but it wasn't until fairly recently that assembly line robots could take the place of human operators. Even today, when the line goes down because of mechanical failure, human experts need to troubleshoot and repair the problem.

Because industrial technologies tend to be hands-on, they have proven to be very useful in classroom instruction. Educators have become highly aware of the many uses of manipulative materials in promoting learning and understanding. From the Language Experience Approach and Math Their Way to Problem Based Instruction and Learning Laboratories, education is replete with theories of learning as a multisensory, interactive process. Industrial technologies were developed to simplify real-world applications for humankind, and they can also bring those real-world applications into the classroom for students.

Industrial Technologies and Education

Perhaps the best example of an early industrial technology is the chalkboard. Mounted on a wall where it could be cleaned and reused daily, this was a breakthrough for educators. Handheld slate boards that had to be carried and distributed around the class were no longer necessary. The chalkboard also provided a new focal point for the classroom, allowing all written communication to be shared with the class. Teachers no longer had to disseminate all information orally, nor did they have to present written lessons individually or to small, huddled groups. Suddenly the classroom seemed more open, and everyone had breathing room to work.

Jump ahead in time and consider the effect that the overhead projector has had on instruction. The chalkboard is now commonplace in the classroom, with its chalk dust and daily cleaning chores. The overhead allows teachers the same convenience of presenting material to the entire room by writing on a reusable surface. The big breakthrough is that teachers can now write assignments on an overhead and never have to turn their backs on the class. Instruction becomes more engaged, with brightly colored transparencies that catch students' attention and explain material in greater visual detail. In some classrooms the chalkboard is relegated to a place for magnets and a projection screen. Technology, in other words, can completely change the way that instruction is delivered to students.

While technologies like these may have been designed specifically for instructional purposes, many industrial technologies used to facilitate learning are not the sole domain of education. Any manmade innovation designed to help us more effectively interact with our environment is a technology. Look in any science laboratory and you quickly see all kinds of equipment adapted for use in instruction: beakers, Bunsen burners, safety goggles, syringes, batteries, measuring tapes, and faucets for running water, to name a few. Consider the tools used in vocational education programs for auto repair, woodworking, and cooking. The tools of each trade are Industrial Age technologies that are necessary for hands-on apprenticeship at the high school level. From elementary grades on up, technology is all around us in the classroom.

Unfortunately, many industrial technologies have been limited to alternative education programs. For the mainstream classroom, lecture, reading, writing, and computation have been the staples of education. Introducing real-world technologies has been perceived as a necessity only for those students who could not function in an environment built around the verbal and logical intelligences. As we have learned more through brain research, though, classroom learning environments have become less centered on verbal and logical models and are more inclusive of technologies that can stimulate all the known paths to learning.

Industrial Technologies and MI Theory

Gardner's theory of multiple intelligences is significant in that it gives teachers a framework in which to identify the appropriate uses of industrial technologies for instruction. Whereas child-centered teachers may have always instinctively included opportunities for building and creating in the classroom, they may now incorporate these activities with greater confidence that they are accommodating all kinds of learners. The integration of industrial technologies into the classroom need no longer be a hit or miss proposition!

The first step in using technology effectively in the classroom is to apply our knowledge of different technologies to Gardner's model. For example, using a lever in a science unit on simple machines at first glance stimulates the kinesthetic path to learning. However, depending on the intended use of the lever in a lesson, it can stimulate a number of other intelligences, too. If the student is expected to determine the correct placement of a fulcrum to lift a textbook off a table using the least amount of energy, the logical intelligence comes into play. If students are asked to identify the different kinds of levers in use around the classroom, it becomes an exercise in logical, musical, and naturalist intelligences as they look for patterns and classify levers by their attributes. The intelligences a technology stimulates are determined by the context in which the technology is used for instruction.

With this in mind, let's consider how different technologies map to each of the intelligences. While Table 4 is by no means exhaustive, it offers examples of nondigital technologies and the intelligences they stimulate.

TABLE 4

Intelligences and Nondigital Technologies

INTELLIGENCE	NONDIGITAL TECHNOLOGIES
Verbal	Pencils, pens, worksheets, textbooks, newspapers, magazines, typewriters, microphones
Logical	Cuisenaire rods, unifix cubes, tangrams, measuring cups, measuring scales, rulers and yardsticks, slide rules, calculators
Visual	Picture books, art supplies, chalkboards, dry erase boards, overhead projectors, slide projectors, TVs, VCRs, cameras, video cameras
Kinesthetic	Construction tools, kitchen utensils, screws, levers, wheels and axles, inclined planes, pulleys, wedges, physical education equipment
Musical	Pattern blocks, puzzles, musical instruments, phonographs, headphones, tape players, tape recorders
Intrapersonal	Journals, diaries, surveys, voting machines, learning centers, children's literature
Interpersonal	Post-it notes, greeting cards, laboratories, telephones, walkie-talkies, intercoms, mail, board games, costumes
Naturalist	Magnifying glasses, microscopes, telescopes, bug boxes, scrap books, sandwich bags, plastic containers
Existential	Art replicas, planetariums, stage dramas, classic literature, classic philosophy, symbols of world religions, simulation games

By keeping in mind the particular properties of each technology, teachers can successfully select those industrial applications that will match learning objectives to the intelligences that thrive in every classroom. For example, in teaching about ancient Greece, teachers may already use many verbal and visual technologies. However, they can expand their students' understanding by including these technologies as well:

- Use hands-on materials to apply the principles developed by ancient Greek mathematicians. (Logical, Kinesthetic)

- Construct working models of simple machines used in daily life in ancient Greece. (Kinesthetic)

- Record a tape of the sounds that would be heard on the streets of ancient Athens, with each student contributing to the recording. (Musical)

- Create fictional journals in which students share their reactions to events that occurred in ancient Greece. (Intrapersonal)

- Design costumes and participate in an improvisation on an important event in Greek history. (Interpersonal, Existential)

- Prepare Greek foods and categorize them based on their taste or ingredients. (Kinesthetic, Naturalist)

- Create a classroom planetarium by devising constellation projections using flashlights and container lids. (Kinesthetic, Existential)

By accommodating a variety of intelligences in your instruction, you can increase your students' comprehension, retention, and recall of material, whether you are building on their long-term understanding or preparing them for standardized testing.

Digital Technologies

The last 30 years have changed the landscape of technology and, indeed, society. The advent of the microcomputer introduced a whole new level of effective, efficient interaction with our environment. Early on, the emphasis was on peripherals that would help us use the microcomputer to accomplish traditional tasks. Light pens, touch pads, and touch screens allowed us to input information into the computer using familiar utensils. At the same time, early educational software was primarily linear in nature, favoring word processing, math, and science applications over more open-ended activities. Simulations had their place in science and social studies software, but the applications tended to be limited by the technology of the time.

Productivity packages offered a different approach to technology use. The combination of word processing, spreadsheet, database, and multimedia presentation software in one suite of digital tools allowed users to apply software to their unique needs. For example, a small business could use a productivity package to keep track of its expenses, profits, and clients. With a little ingenuity, tax records, invoices, and contracts could also be managed using the same software suite.

However, the way an office application suite is used in the classroom is very different from the way it is used in a small business. Word processing and spreadsheet software can easily be used to create and augment research papers and reports on gathered data. Databases can be created to track each student's reading throughout the year or to create mailing labels for a long-term project that requires partners in other parts of the world. Moreover, no one has more fun with multimedia production software than students, as they experiment with new and different ways to present what they have learned. Productivity packages are much more versatile and adaptable than software titles developed around specific content or tasks.

The explosion of the Internet is probably the single event that has done the most to usher in the Digital Age. From electronic mail and gophers to file transfer protocol, synchronous communication, and the World Wide Web, the Internet has made digital technology as vital and immediate as the industrial technologies that preceded it. No longer can computers be categorized simply as business tools or the playthings of math and science scholars. Suddenly, everyone can communicate and access data from around the world using a phone line. The Industrial Age limits of time and space can now be broken by a single keystroke. This new technology has the potential to exponentially improve the quality of life at work, school, and home. Today when we use the word "technology," we are more likely to be referring to Web sites, instant messaging, and electronic mail than to the industrial technologies of the mid-20th century.

Digital Technologies and Education

As schools have tried to keep pace with society and provide students with the skills they will need to compete in tomorrow's job market, they have purchased the hardware and network infrastructure necessary to integrate digital technology into the traditional, Industrial Age classroom. Labs have been set up and acceptable use policies have been put in place to promote the use of these new technologies. Software has been purchased and local area networks built to try to keep up with the quickly changing digital world. Schools are truly on the technology bandwagon.

But where is that bandwagon headed, and how willing are teachers to stay on for the ride if there isn't a sound educational destination? Technology for technology's sake has a shine that loses its luster quickly. School systems have piles of hardware and software that are no longer in use because they didn't live up to their original billing. That, coupled with quickly changing technology, makes investing in digital technology seem like a very risky business. The only way to ensure that emerging technologies are going to be successful in the classroom is to make sure that they are well grounded in educational theory, thoughtfully implemented, and then carefully reflected upon. No theory is more capable of matching technology to the needs of learners than Gardner's model.

Consider how digital technologies map to each of the nine intelligences (Table 5).

TABLE 5

Intelligences and Digital Technologies	
INTELLIGENCE	**DIGITAL TECHNOLOGIES**
Verbal	Keyboards, electronic mail, speech recognition devices, text bridges
Logical	Graphing calculators, FTP clients, gophers, search engines
Visual	Monitors, digital cameras, camcorders, scanners
Kinesthetic	Mouses, joysticks, assistive technologies
Musical	Speakers, CD-ROM discs, CD-ROM players
Intrapersonal	Online forms, real-time projects
Interpersonal	Chats, message boards, instant messengers
Naturalist	Floppy drives, file managers, semantic mapping tools
Existential	MUVEs, virtual reality, virtual communities, blogs, wikis, simulations

Later, we will identify specific kinds of software that stimulate the different intelligences. By mapping available technologies to the nine intelligences, we can maximize the effectiveness of our use of technology in instruction.

How can digital technology stimulate the intelligences? The process is not usually as hands-on as with the Industrial Age technologies. Consider how high school teacher Tronie Gunn developed a lesson for her students on sorting and searching using spreadsheets. Table 6 shows how she is able to address eight of the nine intelligences using a specially structured lesson plan format that carefully maps each element of her lesson to the appropriate intelligences.

TABLE 6

Sorting and Searching Lesson

LESSON TITLE: Sorting and Searching
TEACHER: Tronie Gunn, Westbury High School, Houston, Texas
GRADE LEVEL: 10
SUBJECT(S): Math **TIME FRAME:** 2 1-hour periods

OBJECTIVE(S)	INTELLIGENCES	TECHNOLOGIES	STANDARDS
• Using a spreadsheet, the learners will test standard filters using varied sets of data, comparing each sort for its time and space efficiency.	Verbal Logical Visual Interpersonal Intrapersonal Kinesthetic	Computer lab (Pentium 3 computers), spreadsheets	**NETS for Students:** 1. **Basic Operations and Concepts** • Students demonstrate a sound understanding of the nature and operation of technology systems.

MATERIALS	INTELLIGENCES
Sorting and Algorithmic Analysis Worksheet Overhead transparencies and an erasable marker Playing cards Teach Yourself Data Structures and Algorithms CD Exposure CD Exposure Supplementary Materials CD	Verbal Logical Visual Interpersonal Intrapersonal Kinesthetic

PROCEDURE

	INTELLIGENCES
Preparation Students read a textbook chapter that describes a variety of sorting algorithms that can be used in a spreadsheet. Students have previously used Excel.	Verbal
Activities 1 Provide a brief overview (use a computer projector when applicable) of the 10 kinds of sorts students will study and compare, the types and sizes of data that will be used, and the investigation tools provided.	Verbal Visual Naturalist
Based on this overview, students will be allowed to select their preferred sort for investigation (first-come, first-served).	Intrapersonal

(Continued)

Sorting and Searching Lesson

(Continued)

PROCEDURE	INTELLIGENCES
2 Assign each student a different sort to investigate individually, using the resources provided (you may assign a sort to more than one student if your class size dictates). They may use the following three resources to conduct their investigation:	Visual Musical Naturalist
• The Teach Yourself Data Structures and Algorithms CD provides examples of most of the sorts (in fast or slow motion and for different kinds of data).	Visual Musical Naturalist
• The Exposure Supplementary Materials CD provides visual demonstrations for most of the sorts (using dots or bars).	Logical Musical Naturalist
• The Exposure CD provides a program in chapter 43 that allows a detailed investigation of each of the identified sorts, specifying different types of data and providing the elapsed time required to complete the sort.	Logical Kinesthetic
3 Each student builds an Excel spreadsheet for the algorithm studied. If more than one student investigated a given algorithm, average the results.	Logical Musical Naturalist
Have students use playing cards to demonstrate a working knowledge of how each sort works.	Kinesthetic Musical
As a class, reflect on why some sorts do not work for some data.	Intrapersonal Musical
4 Use an overhead projector and transparencies to report results of the investigations and to facilitate comparisons of the different algorithms.	Interpersonal Logical Musical Naturalist

PRODUCT

Students will complete and submit the Sorting and Algorithmic Analysis Worksheet. Students will demonstrate their understanding of the lesson with playing cards. Students will participate in a class discussion.	Verbal Logical Visual Interpersonal Intrapersonal Kinesthetic

ASSESSMENT

Students will be evaluated on their completion of the Sorting and Algorithmic Analysis Worksheet.	Verbal Logical
Students will be evaluated on their demonstration with playing cards.	Kinesthetic
Students will be evaluated on their participation in the class discussion.	Interpersonal Intrapersonal

(Continued)

Sorting and Searching Lesson

(Continued)

SORTING AND ALGORITHMIC ANALYSIS WORKSHEET

Based on the description and simulations provided, investigate your assigned sort. Use the testing program (from chapter 42) for different data set sizes (500, 1000, 2000, 4000, 8000, 16000, 32000) and different initial data orders (random, ascending, descending). Record the results of your runs on your Excel spreadsheet for comparison. Try to identify the best case, worst case, and average case scenario for your sort. Answer the questions below, and be prepared to demonstrate how your sort works with a set of playing cards. The sorts are as follows:

Dumb Bubble Sort	Smart Bubble Sort
Insertion Sort (with array)	Insertion Sort (with linked list)
Selection Sort	Shell-Metzner Sort
Mergesort	Quicksort
Heapsort	Binary Tree Sort

Algorithm Table: Graphs data set with relationship to its size

Algorithm							
Data Size	500	1000	2000	4000	8000	16000	32000
Random							
Growth	XX						
Sorted							
Growth	XX						
Reverse							
Growth	XX						

1 When the data set size doubles, how does the execution time change for a random list?

2 When the data set size doubles, how does the execution time change for a sorted list?

3 When the data set size doubles, how does the execution time change for a reverse list?

4 Is this sort consistent regardless of the execution time?

5 Compared with other sorts investigated, where does yours rank in speed?

6 What other features might make this sort more or less appropriate in some circumstances? Describe your algorithm in words.

Notice how Tronie's selection of technologies is consistent with the intelligences she wants to stimulate through this lesson. Her objective is succinctly stated and the intelligences are clearly indicated in framing the context for the software and hardware she intends to use. The instructional design of the lesson provides the context for the intelligences she selects, and the intelligences dictate the appropriate technologies. Notice too that she uses both digital and traditional media in her lesson. Her students can look forward to a challenging, stimulating immersion into the world of spreadsheet filters.

Resources for Further Study

Print

Frazier, M., & Bailey, G. (2004). *The technology coordinator's handbook.* Eugene, OR: International Society for Technology in Education.

Heinich, R., Molenda, M., Russell, J. D., & Smaldino, S. (2001). *Instructional media and technologies for learning* (7th ed.). Upper Saddle River, NJ: Prentice Hall.

Kozma, R. B. (Ed.). (2003). *Technology, innovation, and educational change: A global perspective.* Eugene, OR: International Society for Technology in Education.

Morrison, G. R., & Lowther, D. L. (2004). *Integrating computer technology into the classroom* (3rd ed.). Upper Saddle River, NJ: Prentice Hall.

Newby, T. J., Lehman, J., Russell, J., & Stepich, D. A. (1999). *Instructional technology for teaching and learning: Designing instruction, integrating computers, and using media.* Upper Saddle River, NJ: Prentice Hall.

Poole, B. (1997). *Education for an Information Age: Teaching in the computerized classroom.* Columbus, OH: McGraw-Hill.

Schrum, L., & Berenfeld, B. (1997). *Teaching and learning in the Information Age: A guide to educational telecommunications.* Upper Saddle River, NJ: Prentice Hall.

Online

Association for the Advancement of Computing in Education (AACE): **www.aace.org**

Education World: Technology in the Classroom Center: **www.educationworld.com/a_tech/**

Eisenhower National Clearinghouse Online: Implementing Technology: **www.enc.org/topics/edtech/?ls=sn**

Enhancing Multiple Intelligences Through Multimedia: **http://coe.sdsu.edu/eet/Articles/mimultimedia/index.htm**

Howard Gardner on Multiple Intelligences and New Forms of Assessment: **www.glef.org/php/interview.php?id=Art_975&key=037**

MI & Technology: A Winning Combination!:
www.ri.net/RITTI_Fellows/Carlson-Pickering/MI_Tech.htm

Technology and Multiple Intelligences:
http://eduscapes.com/tap/topic68.htm

Reflections

1 How can the ISTE NETS for Students help you to develop well-grounded, technology-based instruction?

2 Which industrial technologies have you used in instruction? Which digital technologies have you used? Do you feel that you need to know more about these technologies than your students before you make them available in your classroom? Why or why not?

3 How does the instructional context help you to determine the intelligences a technology will stimulate?

4 Which domains on the MI wheel did Tronie emphasize in her lesson?

CHAPTER 4

Media Selection

Teachers are avid consumers of all kinds of media. Assorted media are omnipresent in the classroom, and they strongly influence the quality and success of instruction. A lesson presented several times using a variety of media will be delivered differently each time, and stimulate learners in different ways. As consumers of information, we screen everything we take in through the medium in which it is conveyed. The medium may not quite be the message, but it definitely is a significant part of the learning experience. As MI practitioners we already subscribe to an experiential learning model, but how aware are we of the influence that instructional media have on learning?

Instructional Media

When visiting with teachers from different parts of the country, I often ask them to discuss the current state of technology in their buildings. Regardless of their circumstances, one common denominator surfaces as we talk. Teachers feel bound by their access to technology no matter what the technology might be. If a teacher has access to a television connected to her computer so that she can introduce new content to the class, then that is what she will do. Then again, if she has a VGA projector and a demonstration station at the front of a fully equipped lab, she'll be more likely to make use of that setup rather than the TV.

Not everyone, however, is equally well endowed with technology. Educators have a long and storied history of making the most of what they've got. There are still teachers making do with MECC software in an Apple II GS lab! The technology is 20 years old, but it's what they have to work with. Teachers make do.

Most of us have access to technology that lies somewhere between the Apple II GS and today's cutting-edge digital tools. We have choices. Not every lesson needs to make use of the tools most familiar to us. Yes, the overhead projector and a TV/VCR combination will get a workout in most any school. What about the laserdisc library? Most teachers aren't familiar or comfortable enough with it to make it part of their regular instruction. How about spreadsheets and databases? Yes, they are installed on most machines, but many teachers haven't included them in routine classroom use because they're just not comfortable enough with these software tools to do so. Access, comfort level, and training are all important factors in making the most of technology.

Multiple intelligences theory serves as an impetus to challenge the status quo. Once we subscribe to Gardner's theory, we buy into the premise that we are teaching the children, not the curriculum. With this conviction firmly in place it becomes imperative that we look at the different ways we reach children. Traditional media, such as textbooks, are simply not enough. At one time in this country's history we taught the textbook. Today, however, we teach the children. As we become more aware of the different modalities through which we learn, we are in need of ever more ways to accommodate all the different learners in our classrooms. Fifty years ago this would have been a formidable challenge. But this is the Information Age, and technology is developing at exponential rates to help us meet the needs of all learners. It is truly an amazing time to be in education, as advances in brain research and technology merge to reinforce the conviction that all children can learn.

Media and Intelligences

What are the different media and methodologies we have at our disposal? Think about all the different ways you provide learning experiences for your learners. From the beginning of the morning through afternoon dismissal, how do you create instruction for your students? Here are some common media you may use on any given day:

Textbooks	Television
Pencils and paper	Video
Chalkboards	Tape players/tape recorders
Overhead projectors	Magazines
Manipulatives	Newspapers

These tools have been introduced to the classroom over many years as technology has made it possible. With the dawn of the Digital Age, there are entirely new kinds of media:

CD players	Digital references
Laserdiscs	Electronic mail
Blogs	Wikis
Word processing	Web sites
Desktop publishing	Newsgroups
Multimedia presentations	Mailing lists
Spreadsheets	Collaborative projects
Databases	Virtual environments

The media available to educators today is truly impressive. In a traditional approach to intelligence, we might assign digital technologies by intelligence in the manner shown in Figure 6.

FIGURE 6
Intelligences and Various Media

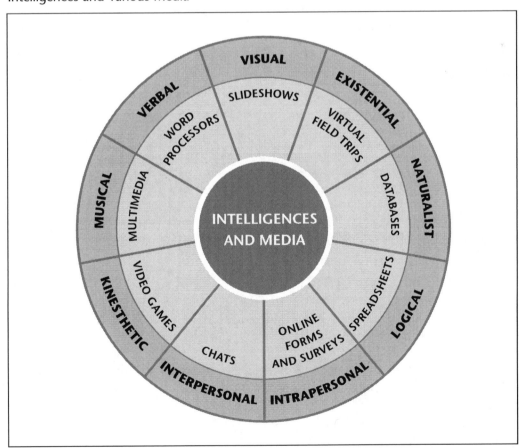

Word processing obviously helps us craft ideas in words, and spreadsheets help us manipulate numbers. But mapping technology to intelligence is not as simple as this surface-level, one-to-one correspondence. Effective media selection is a key component of instructional design. How do we map media to intelligences? It's not so much a matter of identifying the nature of the application itself as it is identifying how the application will be used to meet your instructional objectives.

Selecting Media

To make appropriate media selections, you must first look at your learners. Are they being introduced to new material, are they practicing skills or concepts, or are they reviewing content already taught? What background material have they already covered? Are there prerequisite skills they need to master? What is their ability level with the instructional content?

Second, look at the learning objective. Is it appropriate for your learners? What is to be accomplished by the end of this lesson? How have you structured activities to make this possible? How will you evaluate learner success at the end of the lesson? By answering these four questions you can determine which technologies will match your identified objective. This helps you to narrow down your media choices for the lesson.

Finally, consider the intelligences. Which of the nine will you stimulate in this lesson? Are there additional intelligences from the MI wheel that would help balance your instruction? Which technologies best accommodate these intelligences? Answering these questions will help you focus on the technology or technologies that are most appropriate for your lesson.

The process should always flow in the same direction:

> **Learner > Objective > Intelligences > Technology**

By considering instructional design factors in this order, you can successfully select appropriate media for any lesson in your classroom.

Supporting Intelligences With Technology

Considering the learner and objective will be second nature to most teachers. But how do we consider the intelligences with regard to technology? It is tempting to select the technology you want to use and then make it "fit" the intelligences. However, does that process truly help you identify appropriate strategies, or does it simply allow you to go through the motions to justify your personal preferences? Instead, start with your knowledge of intelligences and consider which media will naturally support them. Elementary teacher Gerry Gontarz has done exactly that in a field trip to a local intertidal zone, as described in Table 7.

TABLE 7

Field Trip to Odiorne Point Lesson

LESSON TITLE: Field Trip to Odiorne Point, Rye, New Hampshire
TEACHER: Gerry Gontarz, Plymouth Elementary School, Plymouth, New Hampshire
GRADE LEVEL: 6
SUBJECT(S): Science   **TIME FRAME:** 1 day

OBJECTIVES(S)	INTELLIGENCES	TECHNOLOGIES	STANDARDS
• Students will demonstrate an understanding of the ecology of a rocky intertidal zone.	Kinesthetic Naturalist Visual Verbal Interpersonal Logical	Journals Pencils Plankton tow Digital microscope with camera Computer Browser Web sites	**NETS for Students:** **3. Technology productivity tools** • Students use technology tools to enhance learning, increase productivity, and promote creativity. • Students use productivity tools to collaborate in constructing technology-enhanced models, preparing publications, and producing other creative works. **5. Technology research tools** • Students use technology to locate, evaluate, and collect information from a variety of sources.

MATERIALS	INTELLIGENCES
Traditional Extra shoes and a change of clothes Journals and notebooks Paper Pencils, markers Large chart paper Plankton tow Student microscopes Microscope slides Cover slips	Kinesthetic Naturalist Visual Verbal Interpersonal Logical

(Continued)

Field Trip to Odiorne Point Lesson

(Continued)

MATERIALS	INTELLIGENCES
Digital Access to the Internet Computer Large-screen monitor for class viewing Digital microscope with camera Moticam (camera) software	

PROCEDURE

Part 1: Intertidal Observation and Discussion
The field trip consists of a visit to Odiorne Point, an intertidal zone in Rye, New Hampshire.

Observation (1–2 hours)
Upon arrival at the intertidal zone, students are put into groups of four to six. Keeping our discussion of ecology in mind and without their notebooks, students descend the rocky coast at low tide and begin. As they observe the intertidal life they are asked to think about connections between both the living and nonliving parts of this ecosystem.

Journal Writing (15–20 minutes)
After one to two hours of exploring, examining, and getting wet, students return to their belongings and immediately begin writing observations in their journals. The observations can be anything observed, even if it does not necessarily reflect the connections between organisms. Reflections about the tactile nature of the experience are also encouraged. (What did it feel like to be in the intertidal zone? Describe the cold water, slippery rocks, and so forth.)

Intelligences: Interpersonal, Verbal, Visual, Naturalist, Kinesthetic

Group Discussion (15–20 minutes)
Students form groups and share their journals. The groups should appoint someone to record their observations. The focus for this session is on trying to make connections between the different life forms as well as between the living and nonliving parts of the environment. Students should answer the following questions when making their connections:

Intelligences: Verbal, Naturalist, Intrapersonal

- Which organisms are the plants?
- Which organisms are the animals?
- Which organisms are the predators?
- Which organisms are the prey?
- Which life forms do you think might be related?
- Are members of other kingdoms present, such as fungi, protists, or monera?
- How are rocks involved in the lives of intertidal organisms?
- How does the energy of the sun literally "flow" through intertidal life?

Intelligences: Verbal, Logical, Naturalist, Interpersonal

Wrap-up (15–20 minutes)
Everyone comes together and shares information that the group recorders have written down. The teacher makes note of the observations on a large piece of chart paper.

Intelligences: Verbal, Interpersonal

(Continued)

Field Trip to Odiorne Point Lesson

(Continued)

PROCEDURE	INTELLIGENCES
Part 2: The Plankton Tow Those familiar with a plankton tow have probably already done a version of this. A plankton tow is a conical mesh net that is fine enough to strain both zooplankton and phytoplankton from water. During the intertidal exploration the teacher demonstrates use of the plankton tow, and then has several students practice in front of the class. The sample is then preserved in a refrigerator or cooler to prevent it from spoiling so that it can be brought back to the classroom.	Logical Kinesthetic Interpersonal Naturalist
The teacher then uses a microscope equipped with a camera (such as the Moticam from Science Kit and Boreal Laboratories, $300). The samples are inserted into the microscope on slides and projected onto a large-screen monitor so that the entire class can view them. Pass out microscopes and have the students view their own samples. Allow students to come up and insert their samples into the monitor-microscope.	Visual Intrapersonal Interpersonal Naturalist
Tell the class that they are looking for both phytoplankton and zooplankton. Point out the differences between these two major groups. What they are looking at represents the basis for all ocean life.	Logical Musical Naturalist
The assignment is to research, using the Internet, how such tiny life forms can be so important. Each student is responsible for handing in a one-page, double-spaced research summary on phytoplankton and zooplankton.	Verbal Logical

PRODUCT	
Journal writing Group work Phytoplankton and zooplankton research	Verbal Intrapersonal Interpersonal Existential Naturalist Kinesthetic Visual Logical

ASSESSMENT	
The following rubrics are used to evaluate student work. **Journal Writing Rubric** A Journal has many detailed observations and reflections of the exploration time. B Journal has some observations and reflections of the exploration time but lacks sufficient detail. C Journal has few observations and reflections of the exploration time. D Journal is incomplete. E Journal was not turned in.	Verbal Intrapersonal

(Continued)

Field Trip to Odiorne Point Lesson

(Continued)

ASSESSMENT	INTELLIGENCES
Group Work Rubric	Interpersonal
A Group members are cooperative and all of the group discussion questions are correctly answered.	Existential
	Naturalist
	Kinesthetic
B Group members are cooperative and almost all of the group discussion questions are correctly answered.	
C Group members are cooperative and most of the group discussion questions are correctly answered.	
D Group members are cooperative and a few of the group discussion questions are correctly answered.	
F Group members do not work well together.	
Phytoplankton and Zooplankton Research Rubric	Visual
A Student work reflects the facts noted above as well as a clear understanding of how the ocean food chain works. Work is free of errors and reflects good research and writing skills.	Logical
B Student work reflects some of the facts noted above but there is still an obvious understanding of the ocean food chain. Work is free of errors and reflects good research and writing skills.	
C Student work reflects some understanding of an ocean food chain. Work reflects that research has been done.	
D Student work does not reflect an understanding of an ocean food chain.	
F Assignment not completed.	

Gerry brings in traditional and digital technologies to help make the most of this field trip experience for his students. He does not try to shoehorn into the lesson plan any digital tools that do not support his instructional outcomes.

Table 8 offers a summary of examples of different technologies appropriate for each intelligence. Many technology choices are available, so educators must choose wisely, selecting to match learning objectives and intelligences to maximize their instructional effectiveness.

TABLE 8

Intelligences and Technologies

INTELLIGENCE	TECHNOLOGIES
Verbal	Textbooks, pencils, worksheets, newspapers, magazines, word processors, electronic mail, desktop publishing tools, Web-based publishing tools, keyboards, speech recognition devices, text bridges
Logical	Cuisenaire rods, unifix cubes, tangrams, measuring cups, measuring scales, rulers and yardsticks, slide rules, graphing calculators, spreadsheets, search engines, directories, FTP clients, gophers, WebQuests, problem-solving tasks, programming languages
Visual	Overhead projectors, televisions, videos, picture books, art supplies, chalkboards, dry erase boards, slideshows, charting and graphing tools, monitors, digital cameras and camcorders, scanners, graphics editors, HTML editors, digital animation/movies
Kinesthetic	Construction tools, kitchen utensils, screws, levers, wheels and axles, inclined planes, pulleys, wedges, physical education equipment, manipulative materials, mouses, joysticks, simulations that require eye-hand coordination, assistive technologies, digital probes
Musical	Pattern blocks, puzzles, musical instruments, phonographs, headphones, tape players, tape recorders, digital sounds, online pattern games, multimedia presentations, speakers, CD-ROM discs, CD-ROM players
Intrapersonal	Journals, diaries, surveys, voting machines, learning centers, children's literature, class debates, real-time projects, online surveys, online forms, digital portfolios with self-assessments
Interpersonal	Post-it notes, greeting cards, laboratories, telephones, walkie-talkies, intercoms, board games, costumes, collaborative projects, chats, message boards, instant messengers
Naturalist	Magnifying glasses, microscopes, telescopes, bug boxes, scrap books, sandwich bags, plastic containers, databases, laserdiscs, floppy drives, file managers, semantic mapping tools
Existential	Art replicas, planetariums, stage dramas, classic literature, classic philosophy, symbols of world religions, virtual communities, virtual art exhibits, virtual field trips, MUDs, blogs, wikis, virtual reality, simulations

Let's take a closer look at each intelligence and the media that will offer appropriate support.

Always well accommodated in the classroom, the **verbal intelligence** can be stimulated even more effectively with modern technologies. Set aside the traditional textbook, pencil, and paper and consider the ways word processing promotes not only composition but also editing and revising in ways that streamline the Writer's Workshop approach. Desktop publishing and Web-based publishing take this idea to new levels of efficacy as students see their work celebrated within the classroom and beyond in the "virtual" world. E-mail is also a wonderful way to promote verbal learning, as students are prompted to request information from and respond to correspondents through written text.

The **logical intelligence** is promoted through activities that require reasoning. These might include processing information provided in a traditional lecture, analyzing data using a spreadsheet, conducting Internet research using a search engine or directory, participating in the problem-solving process of a WebQuest, or even mastering a computer programming language or network protocols.

The **visual intelligence** especially benefits from modern educational technology because there are so many new ways to stimulate this path to learning. While the overhead projector, slide projector, and TV/VCR have been around for 30 years or more, the use of digital slideshows is a newer way to create, manipulate, and present learning in the classroom. Charting and graphing have been made so much easier with software applications such as word processors, draw/paint programs, spreadsheets, and databases, while graphics editors allow us to manipulate any image to meet our needs. Throw in Web site design and construction and recent advances in digital animation and movies, and you can easily see why the visual intelligence is so aptly supported by technology.

The **kinesthetic intelligence** is stimulated by physical interaction with one's environment. When technology is used in instruction, students who learn by manipulating materials can develop a greater understanding of skills and concepts. Diagramming on the board, sorting manipulatives by attributes, participating in a group simulation, or using an adaptive switch to input responses into a computer are all examples of how the kinesthetic intelligence can be accommodated.

The **musical intelligence** is the intelligence of patterns. Technology accommodates it in a variety of ways. For example, playing a tape recording and having students follow the text with books prompts the use of this intelligence. Incorporating digital sounds into a multimedia presentation also accommodates this path to learning. Playing online pattern games such as Mastermind and Concentration can be very musical. Even looking for visual patterns in the classroom or the schoolyard fosters musical thinking.

The **intrapersonal intelligence** is stimulated through activities that bring feelings, values, and attitudes into play. For example, conducting a class debate on an environmental issue, following a real-time expedition through uncharted islands, completing online surveys on an issue being studied in the classroom, completing an online form as a facilitating event for a unit of study, or evaluating one's own digital portfolio full of work from a semester or marking period are all ways to nurture the intrapersonal intelligence.

The **interpersonal intelligence** can be accommodated through class discussion on relevant topics, collaboration on projects that enrich and extend the curriculum, synchronous chat among groups of students or with experts, participation in newsgroups on an assigned topic, and even interaction with mailing lists that allow multiple classes to share ideas and experiences asynchronously.

Organizing and making sense of information in categories and hierarchies stimulates the **naturalist intelligence**. Creating a database to sort and search through data is a wonderful naturalist exercise. Using a laserdisc on weather is an effective way to share scientific phenomena in the classroom. More than any other activity, though, semantic mapping is decidedly the most naturalist. Consider the use of mapping software such as Inspiration to visually map students' understanding of facts and concepts and help them manipulate ideas and tie them together.

The **existential intelligence** is stimulated through learning experiences that reinforce a student's sense of being part of something greater than his or her immediate surroundings. Newspapers, magazines, and virtual communities all help students feel like they belong to something larger than their family or classroom. Virtual art experiences and field trips help students vicariously experience beauty and awe as it exists in the world far beyond the classroom. Blogs and wikis allow learners to interact with one another, sharing and even modifying ideas through an open exchange of information on interactive Web sites. Even online interaction with significant people through interviews and archives can promote the use of the existential intelligence.

The one caveat that has to be made here is that software applications are not so neatly categorized by intelligences. Even though an HTML editing program such as Dreamweaver seems to be a visual tool at first glance, consider the intra- and interpersonal dynamics that come into play as a Web site is formed. Similarly, playing a recorded book in a listening center might be considered a verbal activity rather than a musical task. In fact, it is both. My point is this: the only way to determine the intelligences a technology stimulates is to look at the task the technology is being used to accomplish. The technology itself is not a goal for instruction; it is merely a tool to help you accomplish that goal. It is only when instruction is guided by specific learning objectives that we can see the true nature of any technology and its relationship to the intelligences.

Criteria for Instructional Media

Dr. Sheryl Asen has identified 10 criteria to consider when incorporating technology into instruction. By measuring the use of a technology against these criteria, we can determine how educationally sound it is for instruction.

1 Students are involved in tasks that are broad in scope and challenging. Activities should span a range of experiences and be intellectually demanding.

2 Students, rather than the teacher, have control over the learning process. The teacher serves as more of a guide and coach rather than as a supervisor or administrator.

3 Students work collaboratively and cooperatively. Learning tasks should not be completed in isolation.

4 Students practice and apply communication skills during learning. Learning tasks should promote discussion and interaction.

5 Students participate in varied learning tasks. This includes both variations in the format of the activities and in their objectives.

6 Students have opportunities to address learning tasks in different ways. In this way, different approaches to a presented activity can be explored.

7 Students apply higher order thinking skills through problem-solving tasks. Activities do more than ask students to recall rote facts, terms, and definitions.

8 Students are encouraged to offer varied solutions to a given problem. Standard responses are not the only ones accepted; other answers can be acceptable.

9 Students are encouraged to contribute personal ideas and experience to the learning task. There is validation of student contributions into the learning process.

10 Students are intrinsically motivated by the prescribed learning tasks. Accomplishing the task is rewarding in itself, regardless of the technologies being used.

Note how well Asen's criteria match up with Gardner's intelligences. From the learning objective to formal assessment and at every step in between, multiple intelligences theory can help teachers expand their repertoire of instructional strategies and balance their selection of resources and materials.

Let's return to the process we discussed at the beginning of this chapter. To properly select a medium for instruction, we need to identify the instructional context. To do so, we must we aware of the learner, objective, and intelligences to be stimulated. The process looks like this:

> **Learner > Objective > Intelligences > Technology**

Teachers often take the first step—identifying the learner—for granted. It's just so tempting to assume that one size fits all, and that by aiming for the middle of the class's ability range everyone will achieve some degree of mastery. Why not? That was the ideal of the Industrial Age. But if we truly look at the distribution of intelligences in the classroom it quickly becomes apparent that one size does not fit all. Everyone is capable in his or her own way!

Second, you must know your learning objective and the observable behaviors you want your learners to demonstrate. The activities you select for the lesson should match the learner to the objective. Once you have accomplished this, you can easily identify the intelligences you want to target for the lesson and the most appropriate technology or technologies.

For example, Ms. Donohue is preparing to teach her annual lesson on finding the mean, median, and mode in statistical analysis of data. In considering her learners, she keeps in mind the MI survey she administered at the beginning of the year. This is a predominantly visual group of learners, and they won't pick up these abstract mathematical concepts quickly through rote drill and practice. She considers the intelligences she wants to stimulate in this lesson and identifies the visual, naturalist, and interpersonal as the three to emphasize. After much consideration, she develops a lesson that uses spreadsheets and their associated graphing capabilities to introduce these concepts (Table 9).

TABLE 9

Mean, Median, and Mode Lesson

LESSON TITLE: Mean, Median, and Mode
TEACHER: Donohue
GRADE LEVEL: 4
SUBJECT(S): Math   TIME FRAME: 50 minutes

OBJECTIVE(S)	INTELLIGENCES	TECHNOLOGIES	STANDARDS
• Given a set of data and a spreadsheet, learners will work in pairs to create formulae that will identify the mean, median, and mode.	Naturalist Interpersonal	Spreadsheet	**NETS for Students:** 3. **Technology productivity tools** • Students use technology tools to enhance learning, increase productivity, and promote creativity.
• Given a set of data with identified mean, median, and mode, each pair of learners will create and print a table and graph that represent their findings.	Visual Interpersonal	Spreadsheet	

This is a fictional start of a lesson meant to prompt the reader to think about what the next steps would be in modifying the lesson based on the objectives, technologies, intelligences, and standards. It is not meant to be filled out as an entire lesson using the template.

Proper media selection is a must if multiple intelligences and technology are to be applied effectively in instruction. Note how the objectives and materials correspond to the visual and naturalist intelligences in this example. Of course, the procedure will dictate the interpersonal quality of the lesson. Ms. Donohue's lesson planning is off to a great start.

Resources for Further Study

Print

Alessi, S. M., & Trollip, S. R. (2000). *Multimedia for learning: Methods and development* (3rd ed.). Upper Saddle River, NJ: Allyn & Bacon.

Armstrong, A. (2003). *Instructional design in the real world: A view from the trenches.* Hershey, PA: Information Science Publishing.

Bowe, F. G. (2000). *Universal design in education: Teaching nontraditional students.* New York: Bergin & Garvey.

Ertmer, P. A., & Quinn, J. (2002). *The ID casebook: Case studies in instructional design* (2nd ed.). Upper Saddle River, NJ: Prentice Hall.

Ivers, K. S., & Barron, A. E. (1997). *Multimedia projects in education: Designing, producing, and assessing.* Portsmouth, NH: Libraries Unlimited.

Kozma, R. B. (Ed.). (2003). *Technology, innovation, and educational change: A global perspective.* Eugene, OR: International Society for Technology in Education.

Thorsen, C. (2002). *TechTactics: Instructional models for educational computing.* Upper Saddle River, NJ: Allyn & Bacon.

Online

Case Studies in Instructional Technology and Design:
http://curry.edschool.virginia.edu/go/ITcases/

How Technology Enhances Howard Gardner's Eight Intelligences:
www.america-tomorrow.com/ati/nhl80402.htm#contents

Instructional Design—Robert Gagné, The Conditions of Learning:
www.keele.ac.uk/depts/cs/Stephen_Bostock/docs/atid.htm

Instructional Design and Media Selection:
http://doc.utwente.nl/fid/1431

Instructional Design Theories:
www.indiana.edu/~idtheory/home.html

Media Selection Worksheet:
http://hakatai.mcli.dist.maricopa.edu/authoring/handbook/cs-media.html

Multiple Intelligences and Multimedia:
www.tecweb.org/styles/gardner.html

Reflections

1 Do you agree that objectives and learners need to be considered before the intelligences and technologies? Why or why not?

2 How can ineffective media selection interfere with accommodation of the intelligences in instruction?

3 Conduct a learning materials inventory in your building. Which intelligences are best supported by the technologies you own?

CHAPTER 5

Software Selection

The software market has grown exponentially in the last 20 years as the demand for a wide range of applications has increased. Educational software in particular has become a viable market as educators and parents alike have sought titles that meet the learning needs of children. Because market forces dictate so much of what is published, it is much easier to locate titles by content area and high-interest topic than by the different intelligences.

Categories of Software

To begin the process of selection, consider these categories of software:

Tutorial. Software that teaches concepts and skills and how to apply them

Assessment. Software that evaluates student mastery of specified skills and concepts through appropriate tasks

Guided Practice. Software that provides practical exercises and drills with support, interaction, and feedback

Independent Practice. Software that requires users to apply specific skills to reach an identified goal

Heuristic. Software that presents users with problem-solving challenges that can be completed using more than one strategy

Simulation. Software that simulates complex macro- and microprocesses

Productivity. Software used for writing, composing, organizing, sorting, calculating, drawing, painting, and publishing

Software and Intelligences

Many different kinds of software are available to educators. Knowing the common-sense categories can help you assess the strengths and weaknesses of your software library. Looking at software by the intelligences they stimulate can further reveal which paths to learning you already support through software.

It is also useful to evaluate software based on the kinds of cognitive processing it stimulates. For this purpose, there is no better guide than Bloom's taxonomy. This classification of learning skills, first proposed in the 1950s, has been among the most influential educational theories in the past half-century, and has been applied in numerous ways. Bloom's taxonomy consists of six levels, ranging from lower level (Knowledge, Comprehension, and Application) to higher level cognitive processes (Analysis, Synthesis, and Evaluation). Table 10 shows the correlation of each of the software categories with Gardner's intelligences and Bloom's taxonomy.

TABLE 10

SOFTWARE CATEGORY	INTELLIGENCES	BLOOM
Software by Intelligence and Level of Thinking		
Tutorial	Logical Verbal	Knowledge Comprehension
Assessment	Logical Verbal	Knowledge Comprehension
Guided Practice	Logical Verbal Musical Naturalist	Knowledge Comprehension Application
Independent Practice	Logical Verbal Musical Naturalist Intrapersonal	Knowledge Comprehension Application Analysis
Heuristic	Logical Verbal Musical Naturalist Intrapersonal Interpersonal	Knowledge Comprehension Application Analysis Synthesis
Simulation	Logical Verbal Musical Naturalist Intrapersonal Interpersonal Visual Existential	Knowledge Comprehension Application Analysis Synthesis
Productivity	Logical Verbal Musical Naturalist Intrapersonal Interpersonal Visual Existential Kinesthetic	Knowledge Comprehension Application Analysis Synthesis Evaluation

Certainly, software can be designed that addresses more intelligences or higher levels of thinking than those identified in Table 10, but in isolation these are the minimum attributes for each software category.

Consider the implications of breaking down software in this way:

- **Tutorial** and **assessment** applications address at least the logical and verbal intelligences at the lowest levels of Bloom's taxonomy. Can these applications involve visuals, auditory effects, and other extras? Of course. But look at the typical processes that learners must go through to accomplish a task: they tend to be very linear and dependent on a learner's ability to recall, restate, or identify.

- **Guided** and **independent practice** applications bring in the musical, naturalist, and intrapersonal intelligences as students are invited to find and apply patterns and make sense of content in different contexts—thereby employing Bloom's application and analysis skills.

- **Heuristic** and **simulation** applications add the emotional intelligences: interpersonal and intrapersonal. In problem solving, this allows for the use of individual values and attitudes and the opportunity to participate in group collaboration. In simulations, students can also be engaged through the visual and existential intelligences as they place themselves in a virtual environment and apply their knowledge and skills to successfully complete tasks. Both heuristic and simulation applications promote Bloom's synthesis level of thinking, as students generate possible solutions to identified challenges.

- **Productivity** software includes all the intelligences, including the kinesthetic, as students manipulate various tools to create their own original products. When students respond to one another's work, it stimulates the existential intelligence as well as the evaluation level of Bloom's taxonomy. Productivity applications can be most useful in accommodating all the intelligences in your classroom.

Of course, the intelligences stimulated by any software are dependent on the context in which an application is used. A tutorial application can be used to stimulate a number of intelligences if it is used in concert with other instructional tasks. Likewise, a productivity tool such as a word processor can be used simply to stimulate the verbal intelligence to show student understanding of vocabulary words at Bloom's knowledge level. Context is the defining criterion in applying Gardner's work. The categories I have suggested here are meant in general terms only and can be modified based on your particular instructional design.

On the other hand, there is a temptation to be all-inclusive in matching teaching materials to the intelligences. Any strategy or application can accommodate any intelligence with enough contortions and forced connections. But remember, Gardner's theory describes these pathways to learning in their natural state as they actually function in human cognition. The connections we make to the intelligences should be just as natural and logical as Gardner's, not forced or contrived. A forced connection is self-defeating, as students will be unlikely to see it or benefit from it, and you'll eventually have to revisit the entire skill or concept. Forced connections come from trying to justify the ways you've always taught and the materials you've always used. Why bother? Once you start down the road of integrating MI theory into instruction, you make an implicit commitment to yourself to be honest, to be open to new possibilities, and to be willing to change.

Conducting an MI Software Inventory

The best way to determine the strengths of your existing applications and how you might use them is to take a software inventory. Get a master list of software titles available to you from your technology or curriculum coordinator and plug them into a table that considers each application by the intelligences it addresses. See Table 11 for an example.

TABLE 11

Multiple Intelligences Software Inventory			
INTELLIGENCES	**SOFTWARE**		
	Accel. Reader	**Kid Pix**	**TimeLiner**	**Oregon Trail**
Verbal	✔	✔		
Logical	✔		✔	✔
Visual		✔	✔	✔
Kinesthetic		✔		✔
Musical		✔	✔	✔
Intrapersonal		✔		✔
Interpersonal				✔
Naturalist			✔	✔
Existential		✔		✔

It is important to check off only those intelligences that are primarily stimulated by each application. Accelerated Reader, for example, primarily stimulates the verbal and logical intelligences through its emphasis on reading comprehension and its multiple choice quiz format. TimeLiner, on the other hand, stimulates the logical and visual intelligences through timeline creation, the musical intelligence through the patterns that can be traced in the timeline, and the naturalist intelligence through the different kinds of categories by which timeline events can be organized. Certainly Kid Pix could have a logical, interpersonal, or naturalist component to it if the lesson is designed to accommodate those specific intelligences, but that isn't what you're evaluating in this inventory. The purpose of this inventory is to determine the intelligences that each application supports *on its own merits*, before instruction takes place. When you have completed your MI software inventory, you will be able to identify those intelligences that need to be considered in future software purchases.

Another way to evaluate software is through its content, interface, design, and documentation features.

Content

- Do the learning objectives supported by the software go beyond the lower levels of Bloom's taxonomy?

   Is the software geared toward skill, drill, and recall, or are students challenged to use the material in new and different ways to practice mastery?

- Does the content addressed in the software lend itself to uses across the curriculum?

   For example, does a mathematics application solely address an isolated math skill or does it apply to other areas of your curriculum?

- Does the content lend itself to the perspective of several different intelligences?

   Is it strictly a linear, logical application, or can visual and existential learners appreciate its content too?

- Is the content adaptive to different intelligences, even those not addressed in the software itself?

   What are the possibilities for extending the content and skills addressed into other classroom activities?

- Do the software's explanations, definitions, and directions accommodate different intelligences?

   Is there more than one way to learn in and about the application, or are the directions optimal only for verbal or logical learners?

Interface

- Does the software intuitively adapt to users with different intelligence strengths?

   Can the application make adjustments based on the kinds of input it receives from students, or does it simply track ability level?

- Are there visual, auditory, and kinesthetic components to the software?

   Will students be able to navigate with ease through a variety of different kinds of prompts, or do the prompts tend to be strictly visual?

- Do the support and help functions accommodate students of different intelligences?

   When students look for assistance within the application itself, is it always verbal or logical, or are there examples for kinesthetic and naturalist learners too?

- Do the metaphors used to explain software functions address varied intelligences?

   Are there only icons and buttons, or are other familiar contexts used, such as storybooks, playgrounds, neighborhoods, and families?

- Is navigation through the software global and open-ended rather than linear and skill based?

   Do students have lots of choices, and can they make them in any order they choose without hindrance?

Design

- Is the software interactive and responsive to student input?

   Do intelligences become activated through student interaction with the application?

- Does the design support a variety of intelligences?

   Are there multiple ways to successfully accomplish tasks in the application, or must everyone use the same strategies and orientation?

- Is there evidence of scaffolding to support learners as they strengthen less developed intelligences?

   Does the application provide support for students who may not feel as confident or comfortable completing certain kinds of tasks because of their personal distribution of intelligences?

- Are there ways to extend the learning experience from the software into the classroom?

   Can you adapt the application's instructional strategies into classroom lessons that will reinforce what students are practicing?

- If assessment takes place, does it match the intelligences used in instruction?

   If there is testing or record keeping of skill mastery, does it provide assessment tasks that use the same intelligences targeted by the instruction itself?

Documentation

- Do the manual and teacher support materials address different intelligences?

   Is there explicit treatment of different student orientations to learning in the support materials that come with the application?

- Do the manual and teacher support materials acknowledge higher order thinking skills?

   Are there synthesis and evaluation tasks included among the application's learning activities?

- Are extension activities included that can help address additional intelligences beyond the limitations of the software?

   Does the documentation include lesson plans or activity sheets that can help you transfer digital experiences into classroom activities?

- Are there recommended resources you can use to further enrich and extend the use of the software across the intelligences?

   Does the software offer links to online activities, print materials, or additional software titles?

- Are there suggestions for alternative assessment tasks?

   If the application provides verbal and logical assessment tasks, does the documentation also suggest other ways to assess student learning?

Of course, many software companies are not yet addressing the distribution of intelligences across a student population, so you probably will not see specific references to multiple intelligences per se. But with your own MI awareness, you can identify the elements of well-designed software that accommodate multiple intelligences no matter how the publisher packages them.

You will also want to know which software titles have already been classroom tested and are popular choices of teachers around the country for instructional use. Table 12 provides a listing of software applications by intelligence that have been rated the best by educators in North America. Thanks to the members of the Tech Coordinators list (**www.thesnorkel.org/people.htm**), the National Association for the Education of Young Children's list (**http://capwiz.com/naeyc/mlm/**), the Early Childhood Educator's list (**www.umaine.edu/eceol/**), and the Connected Teacher mailing list (**www.classroom.com/community/email/**), all of whom submitted titles for inclusion in this table.

TABLE 12

Software Application by Intelligence

INTELLIGENCE	APPLICATION	PURCHASING INFORMATION
Verbal	Bailey's Book House	www.riverdeep.net/products/early_learning/baileys_bh.jhtml
	Clicker	www.cricksoft.com/us/products/clicker/default.asp
	Co:Writer	www.donjohnston.com/catalog/cow4000d.htm
	Write: Out Loud	www.donjohnston.com/catalog/writoutd.htm
	Microsoft Word	http://office.microsoft.com/home/office.aspx?assetid=FX01085799
Logical	Graph Club	www.tomsnyder.com/products/product.asp?SKU=GRPV20
	Microsoft Excel	http://office.microsoft.com/home/office.aspx?assetid=FX01085800&CTT=6&Origin=EC010963431033
	Millie's Math House	www.riverdeep.net/products/early_learning/millies_mh.jhtml
	Math Realm	www.cogtech.com
	Prime Time Math	www.sheppardsoftware.com/pmath1.htm
Visual	Flash	www.macromedia.com/software/flash/
	Golly Gee Blocks	www.gollygee.com
	Kid Pix	www.kidpix.com
	Microsoft PowerPoint	http://office.microsoft.com/home/office.aspx?assetid=FX01085797
	NIH Image	http://rsb.info.nih.gov/nih-image/index.html
	Adobe Photoshop	www.adobe.com/products/photoshop/

(Continued)

Software Application by Intelligence

(Continued)

INTELLIGENCE	APPLICATION	PURCHASING INFORMATION
Kinesthetic	CyberStretch	www.cyberstretch.com
	IntelliTools	www.intellitools.com
	Lego Mind Storms	www.pldstore.com/pld/catalog.cfm?dest=dir&linkid=9&linkon=section
	Mavis Beacon	www.broderbund.com/Product.asp?OID=4148830&SC=0190594095&CID=249
	Probeware	www.teamlabs.com
Musical	Cubase	www.steinberg.net/ProductPage_sb.asp?Product_ID=2014&Langue_ID=7
	Finale	www.finalemusic.com
	Introduction to Patterns	http://sunburst-store.com/cgi-bin/sunburst.storefront/40e691b60c7f9a7b2717d00b8932072e/Product/View/8772
	Sibelius	www.sibelius.com/cgi-bin/home/home.pl
	Thinkin' Things	www.riverdeep.net/products/thinkin_things/index.jhtml
Intrapersonal	Choices, Choices	www.tomsnyder.com/products/product.asp?SKU=CHOCHO
	Decisions, Decisions	www.tomsnyder.com/products/product.asp?SKU=DECDEC
	Feelings	www.cdgarden.com/main/software/mw/feelings.htm
	Forrest Center Stage	www.orcca.com/MMProd.htm#Forrest
	Perseus	www.perseus.com
Interpersonal	Dreamweaver	www.macromedia.com/software/dreamweaver/
	ICQ	http://web.icq.com
	Instant Messenger	www.aim.com/index.adp
	MMPI	www.psychscreen.com/singletest/mmpia.html
	Net Meeting	www.microsoft.com/windows/netmeeting/

(Continued)

INTELLIGENCE	APPLICATION	PURCHASING INFORMATION
Software Application by Intelligence *(Continued)*		
Naturalist	Chime Pro and ChemScape	www.mdli.com/products/framework/chimepro/index.jsp
	FileMaker Pro	www.filemaker.com
	IHMC Concept Map Software	http://cmap.ihmc.us/
	Inspiration/ Kidspiration	www.inspiration.com
	Stella	www.iseesystems.com (iedszc45hzv1yp45d0fb4c55)/index.aspx
	TimeLiner	www.tomsnyder.com/products/productdetail.asp?PS=TIMV50
Existential	ArtSpace	www.mprojects.wiu.edu/artspace.shtml
	Geodesy	www.bgrg.com/geodesy/
	Neighborhood Map Machine	www.tomsnyder.com/products/product.asp?SKU=NEIV20
	SimCity	http://simcity.ea.com
	Trudy's Time and Place House	www.riverdeep.net/products/edmark_house_series/trudys_time_place.jhtml

The PEP Model

Regardless of the titles you select for instruction, the proof comes in the way they are utilized in instruction. A software application should not be an end unto itself. It should be part of a larger instructional approach that will help address a variety of intelligences in your classroom. This means you will want to set a context for using the software prior to introducing it to students, and create follow-up activities that extend and enrich the learning experiences it provides. This approach—offering presoftware activities, followed by learning experiences with the software, and ending with postsoftware activities that allow for accommodation of multiple intelligences—will be referred to here as the PEP model (Presoftware, Experience, Postsoftware). Putting the model into practice can come in many shapes and sizes, but the intent is always the same: to integrate the technology into your instruction so thoroughly that it becomes a vital piece in the learning process.

Consider Accelerated Reader. It's quite easy to have the software in place and tell your students to read books and take quizzes, relying on the software to keep track of each student's performance. But that leaves the use of Accelerated Reader as an extraneous task in your classroom that exists on its own without any true tie-in to the meaningful learning you want to provide for your students each day. However, incorporating Accelerated Reader in your curriculum using the PEP model suddenly provides for all kinds of meaningful connections. Here's how you can use the PEP model with Accelerated Reader:

Presoftware. Each month, identify a genre for students to read. Discuss the characteristics of the genre and have your librarian put Accelerated Reader titles that fit this genre on loan to your classroom. Work with students to plan a cumulative activity at the end of the month that will celebrate this genre. Perhaps videotaping book discussions or asking each student to dress as a character from a specific book in the genre would be appropriate. Students might even like designing their own Accelerated Reader quizzes for a book of their choice.

Experience. Have students select titles from the classroom collection and complete Accelerated Reader quizzes when they are done reading them. Continue studying the genre in class.

Postsoftware. Complete the culminating task you and the class agreed on at the beginning of the month. Pass out Accelerated Reader certificates indicating the points each student earned during the process. Review the genre and offer an extension activity in which groups of students work on writing stories in that genre.

Notice in Table 13 how a decidedly verbal and logical software application can be easily adapted for a variety of intelligences simply by writing a lesson plan using the PEP model.

TABLE 13

Example of Planning Using PEP

PRESOFTWARE	EXPERIENCE	POSTSOFTWARE
Identify the genre	Read books in the genre	Design original AR quizzes
Identify cumulative activity	Complete AR quizzes	Pass out AR points

Table 14 shows how Ms. Mannas sets up software applications within the context of a larger lesson to provide rich, meaningful learning that will transfer across intelligences.

TABLE 14

Multimedia Presentation on Animal Dissection Lesson

LESSON TITLE: Multimedia Presentation on Animal Dissection
TEACHER: Susan Mannas, St. Theresa School, Austin, Texas
GRADE LEVEL: 5
SUBJECT(S): Science   **TIME FRAME:** 14 45-minute periods

OBJECTIVE(S)	INTELLIGENCES	TECHNOLOGIES	STANDARDS
• All fifth-grade students will develop and show a HyperStudio multimedia presentation comparing and contrasting four animals they dissected in science class.	Verbal Musical Logical Naturalist Interpersonal Visual Intrapersonal	Computer Scanner CD burner HyperStudio Internet Explorer Word	**NETS for Students:** **5. Technology research tools** • Students use technology to locate, evaluate, and collect information from a variety of sources.

MATERIALS	INTELLIGENCES
Science binder with dissection information, Internet resources sheet, grading rubric	Verbal Visual Logical Musical Naturalist Intrapersonal

PROCEDURE	
Preparation Students have spent several months in science class dissecting four animals—a worm, grasshopper, starfish, and squid. They took many notes as they learned about these animals. A rubric was created that cited the information to be included in the presentation. Students also spent time prior to this assignment learning how to use HyperStudio.	
Activities *Day 1* Go over the rubric.	Visual Logical Verbal Naturalist
Days 2–4 Have students build skeleton pages and work on the organization of the HyperStudio stack and navigational buttons.	Visual Logical Verbal Naturalist

(Continued)

Multimedia Presentation on Animal Dissection Lesson

(Continued)

PROCEDURE	INTELLIGENCE
Day 4 Introduce Web sites from which graphics will be collected. Teach students the correct citation of references under the image that they use and its inclusion on their credits page.	Visual Verbal Logical
Day 5 Scan "squid ink" pictures. (When the students dissected the squid, some of the squid still had ink in them. The students were allowed to create pictures with this ink. On Day 5 we scan the pictures and place them in a shared folder so students can include these pictures in their projects.)	Visual Naturalist
Days 2–10 Students build their stacks. The stacks include the topics from the rubric.	Verbal Musical Logical Naturalist Interpersonal Visual Intrapersonal
Day 11 Students are reminded to check their stacks to make sure they have included the rubric topics. They check their navigation and are finally allowed to add sound. (If students are allowed to add sound as they go, some won't get the "meat" of their project done. They will spend the whole time focusing on sound.)	Musical
Day 12 Students add their finishing touches.	Intrapersonal
Days 13–14 Students present their work.	Interpersonal Visual

PRODUCT	
Students will create and show a HyperStudio multimedia presentation comparing and contrasting four animals they dissected in science class.	Verbal Musical Logical Naturalist Interpersonal Visual Intrapersonal

ASSESSMENT	
A rubric will be used to evaluate the presentations.	Logical Verbal Visual Naturalist

The two presentation days are scheduled with the classes involved, and parents are invited to view their child's work. A CD containing the class presentations is burned and used in the library as a reference source.

Integrating a software application into instruction can be so seamless a part of the process that students naturally use it in learning and demonstrating understanding. The PEP model can help you achieve this kind of second-nature technology use in the classroom.

Resources for Further Study

Print

Aldrich, C. (2003). *Simulations and the future of learning: An innovative (and perhaps revolutionary) approach to e-learning.* Hoboken, NJ: Pfeiffer.

Armstrong, S., Chen, M., George Lucas Educational Foundation, & Lucas, G. (2002). *Edutopia: Success stories for learning in the Digital Age.* Hoboken, NJ: Jossey-Bass.

Bitter, G., & Pierson, M. (2004). *Using technology in the classroom* (6th ed.). Upper Saddle River, NJ: Allyn & Bacon.

Carlson, G. (2004). *Digital media in the classroom.* Gilroy, CA: CMP Books.

Morrison, G. R., & Lowther, D. L. (2004). *Integrating computer technology into the classroom* (3rd ed.). Upper Saddle River, NJ: Prentice Hall.

St. Laurent, A. M. (2004). *Understanding open source and free software licensing.* Sebastopol, CA: O'Reilly.

Velgos, T. (1999). *Evaluating educational software: An educator's guide for classrooms, labs, and libraries.* Manhattan, KS: Master Teacher.

Online

Activating the Multiple Intelligences: Software Ideas:
www.chariho.k12.ri.us/curriculum/MISmart/MISoftwr.htm

Implementing Multiple Intelligences and Learning Styles in Distributed Learning/IMS Projects:
www.tecweb.org/styles/imslsindl.pdf

Inclusion of Gardner's Multiple Intelligences Across the Curriculum in the 21st Century Classroom: Leaving No Student out of the Learning Loop:
www.nssa.us/nssajrnl/20_1/html/Multiple_Intelligences_Mbuva.htm

Integrating Technology in Multiple Intelligences:
www.casacanada.com/multech.html

Multiple Intelligences and Technology:
www.exceptionalcomputing.com/Curriculum%20pdf/multinte.pdf

Software—Multiple Intelligences:
http://db.itrc.ucf.edu/Software01/intel.html

The Software Trap:
http://staffdevelop.org/softwaretrap.html

Reflections

1 "A forced connection is self-defeating, as students will be unlikely to see it or benefit from it, and you'll eventually have to revisit the entire skill or concept." Do you agree with this statement, which appeared earlier in this chapter? Why or why not? What has your experience been in making connections for students?

2 What titles would you add to the recommended software list presented in this chapter?

3 Take an inventory of your school software library. Which categories of software does your collection emphasize? Which categories are not well represented? Which intelligences are best addressed by the titles in your software collection?

4 What would Susan Mannas' PEP chart look like for the lesson presented in Table 14?

6

Modifying Existing Lessons

One of the appealing features of Gardner's theory is that it confirms so much of the work teachers already do in the classroom. Good teachers have been instinctively catering to different intelligences without even knowing of the MI model. Presenting Gardner's theory to teachers is a pleasure because his work validates so many good things they already do. This makes for a sound marriage of theory and practice, because teachers are immediately ready to take a look at their classroom-tested lessons and units and superimpose them on the MI model. It sounds easy enough, right? But you'd be surprised how working through this process raises as many questions as it answers! To make it easier to move from theory to practice, we will look at a process for modifying existing lessons that I call the POMAT approach: Procedure, Objective, Materials, Assessment, and Technology.

A Rationale for Modifying Existing Lessons

For the last half-century, teachers have come to expect textbook publishers and curriculum marketers to put together prepackaged instructional programs that are a combination of salesmanship, structure, and resources. While many reform movements have bemoaned a situation in which the commercial tail is wagging the educational dog, teachers have, in fact, grown quite accustomed to having a prepackaged program in place that they can borrow from and refer to as needed. It's convenient and it saves time. Moreover, it's familiar after five decades; it's comfortable. Gardner, on the other hand, does not advocate the prepackaging of MI theory. MI theory recognizes the unique nature of each individual learner, and developing lessons based on this theory requires a blend of the teacher's personal instructional style with the particular combination of student MI profiles present in any given class. That's not to say that companies are *not* trying to package and sell an "MI approach" to instruction. If they can sell it, they'll market it! It simply means that this prepackaged approach may not be appropriate for effective instruction.

Having said this up front, I know that teachers interested in incorporating MI theory into their curriculum typically analyze and revise existing lessons or units with good intentions and a certain amount of uncertainty:

- Will I have to revise my objectives?

- How do I decide which intelligences to employ?

- Should I incorporate all the intelligences into a lesson?

The answers are not at all clear-cut or obvious once you start looking at your own work.

First, we should agree on a basic rationale for modifying existing instruction: teachers should edit and revise existing lessons and units with the idea of maximizing the number of intelligences accommodated. This should not be an exercise in documenting the intelligences that your lessons and units already address. To simply categorize existing lessons by the intelligences they accommodate is to spend time you don't have validating lessons you don't intend to change. The only common-sense reason for making modifications based on MI is to take lessons you already know and love and improve them by making additional connections for all your students.

We should also have a working definition of what it means to accommodate, stimulate, or otherwise employ an intelligence in a lesson. Exercising an intelligence by definition means that an activity utilizes that intelligence for the explicit purpose of instruction. For example, the fact that students talk with one another while completing a lab experiment is not proof that they are exercising their verbal intelligence. Talking while working is not in and of itself supportive of the instructional outcome. On the other hand, having students work together to brainstorm possible solutions as part of a creative problem-solving activity contributes to the learning outcome of the lesson. It is by definition an accommodation of the verbal intelligence. Another example is Gardner's humorous anecdote of being welcomed into a kindergarten classroom where he observed children crawling on their hands and knees, yelping and howling. When he asked the teacher about the activity, Gardner was informed that the children were exercising their kinesthetic intelligence. Unimpressed, Gardner responded that this was not kinesthetic intelligence, but merely a group of children crawling on the floor and howling like wolves! Keep this story in mind as you identify intelligences in existing lessons.

It is important to remember that it is not necessary or even advisable to try to accommodate all the intelligences in any one lesson. Trying to work all nine intelligences into a single lesson usually results in a contrived, chaotic mess, with students unable to benefit from the resulting saturation of inputs and experiences. Instead, you should expect to integrate no more than three to five intelligences into one lesson. The most appropriate intelligences to target will become evident as you work with an existing lesson and should flow naturally from the content of your plan. This is important because children need to see natural, obvious connections between the intelligences if they are going to truly benefit from your efforts. If your lesson tries to force an intrapersonal connection that just doesn't flow with the rest of the lesson, it will throw students off rather than help them understand. In short, if the introduction of a new intelligence into an existing lesson doesn't fit naturally and easily into your plan, omit it. When in doubt, leave it out!

As for the proper design of an MI lesson, start with a clear objective. Continually refer back to that objective to make sure that you are staying on course as you build the rest of the lesson. For an existing lesson, this may mean modifying the original objective slightly to make room for additional outcomes. With a clear objective in place, you can then identify the intelligences you want to include in your lesson. There should be an obvious, natural connection between any intelligence you choose to include and your objective. Finally, use your objective and list of intelligences to determine the technologies (if any) you would like to employ in the lesson. Not every lesson will benefit from the use of technology, and knowing when it is and is not appropriate comes with practice and experience. As you start the process of modifying lessons, your purpose is to help students reach your stated objective by incorporating technologies that stimulate the target intelligences.

The POMAT Method

The rote practice of identifying the objective, intelligences, and technologies for each lesson can quickly devolve into a going-through-the-motions process in which you no longer use a critical eye. From my own experience, I know that after creating a few lessons in this way it's easy to fall into a pattern of using similar-sounding objectives with familiar intelligences and favorite technology applications, lesson after lesson. People are, after all, creatures of habit and it's hard to look at every new lesson with a fresh eye. For this reason, I have developed the POMAT approach (Procedure, Objective, Materials, Assessment, Technology) to modifying existing lessons. The POMAT process breaks up the lesson revision process into five steps that require you to think about how well your lesson maps out.

The POMAT approach is based on the notion of "backward planning," developed by Grant Wiggins and Jay McTighe, from the view of the teacher-practitioner. The teacher first looks at a lesson's procedure, and then maps back through the objective, materials, and assessment to determine a consistency of purpose. If the actual flow of a lesson nicely matches the objective and assessment, the lesson plan is soundly designed and will bring maximum instructional success. If a lesson is inconsistent in any of its critical components, the POMAT process will identify gaps and weaknesses that the teacher can then address. The entire procedure is designed to examine a lesson's consistency within the context of the nine intelligences. Here are the five steps of POMAT:

1 **Procedure.** Without looking at any other part of the existing lesson, go directly to the procedure and make notes on each prescribed activity and the intelligences it accommodates. For example, if students are asked to select a type of bridge from a previous lesson to employ in their design, you could note the naturalist intelligence (the intelligence of categories and hierarchies) on the POMAT chart (see Table 15). If students are then asked to calculate the dimensions of a bridge they are to build, you might note on the POMAT chart that this stimulates the logical intelligence. Complete this process for the entire lesson's procedure, noting any and all intelligences that are accommodated.

2 **Objective.** Now go to the beginning of your lesson plan and examine your stated objective. Note on the POMAT chart which intelligences seem to fit this objective. For instance, if the objective states that the learner will construct a bridge 3 feet in length that will allow a 12-pound remote-control truck to cross safely 2 feet off the floor, you may note that it will accommodate the logical and kinesthetic intelligences. Be sure to note only the intelligences the objective clearly accommodates.

3 **Materials.** With the procedure and objective reviewed, you can now look at the list of materials you have generated for the lesson. Which intelligences do these materials stimulate? Note on the POMAT chart that the building supplies and hand tools accommodate the logical, visual, and kinesthetic intelligences.

4 **Assessment.** Now, look at your assessment plan. Is it consistent with the procedure, objective, and materials in the intelligences it utilizes? Is there a clear agreement between the objective, materials, procedure, and assessment in terms of the intelligences addressed? In the case of the bridge construction lesson, testing the bridge by rolling the 12-pound truck over it is the test of choice. It is practical, verifiable, and an exciting culminating event for the lesson. If your assessment matches well with your objective and the intelligences you have identified throughout the lesson, you're on solid ground!

5 **Technology.** Finally, review the POMAT chart you have created and determine which technologies, if any, should be included. Most likely you are already employing certain industrial technologies in the lesson. But what about digital technologies? Is this a good activity for introducing probeware? If you project a spreadsheet on the wall and fill it with the data for each bridge the class has constructed, will that be an appropriate use of technology? Or maybe you could use a digital camera to take pictures of the students at work so that the class can work on a multimedia presentation of the experience. With sufficient planning, you could even invite other classes to participate in an online competition to build a bridge that best meets the lesson objective, and compare results and data. Where this lesson fits in your overall curriculum will determine which uses of technology are most appropriate and effective.

The CD-ROM that accompanies this book contains a blank POMAT template for your use. Table 15 shows the five POMAT steps for a culminating lesson in a unit on bridges.

TABLE 15

The POMAT Chart

INTELLIGENCES	POMAT				
	Procedure	*Objective*	*Materials*	*Assessment*	*Technology*
Verbal					
Logical	✔	✔	✔	✔	✔
Visual	✔		✔		✔
Kinesthetic	✔	✔	✔		✔
Musical					
Intrapersonal				✔	
Interpersonal	✔				
Naturalist	✔			✔	
Existential					
NOTES	Organizing, building, measuring, problem solving, working in groups	Problem solving and building	Hand tools, rulers, balsa wood, nails, screws, safety goggles, information books, paper, pencils	Driving 12-pound remote control truck over bridge; identifying the best bridge designs	Hand tools, rulers, nails, screws, remote control trucks

Analyzing your existing lessons using the POMAT method will help you quickly identify areas of strength in your lesson. This bridge construction task, for example, is a logical, problem-solving task with visual and kinesthetic implications for the learner. There's a clear interpersonal dimension to the task, and students must organize and categorize as they go. But look where the lesson comes up empty: for all the chatter that will likely fill the room as the students build their bridges, there's no direct link between the stated lesson objective and the verbal intelligence. Also, for all the patterns discernible in the design of bridges, and for as much aesthetic beauty as they can add to the environment, neither the musical or existential intelligences have instructional connections here. Picture a child in your class who is very verbal but has a hard time generating effective solutions to problems, or a student who has strong personal convictions and is preoccupied with the effect of bridges on the surrounding landscape. As creative and hands-on as this lesson is, it misses the opportunity to connect with these students. If you have a significant number of students who are very strong in these intelligences, you might consider modifying the objective and procedures accordingly.

From this summary of the POMAT exercise, which digital application might be the most appropriate to incorporate in this lesson: probeware, a spreadsheet program, presentation software, or an online collaborative project? Probeware is a catch-all term for an array of tools that allow students to record data and see digital representations of their experiments. It clearly has both visual and logical applications, two intelligences that the task already targets. If you wish to bolster the visual component of this lesson, probeware would be a good choice. A spreadsheet program, such as Excel, is great for stimulating the logical and naturalist intelligences and for making connections to the visual intelligence with a graph or chart. If you would like to reinforce the visual, logical, and naturalist intelligences, Excel is clearly a good choice. Multimedia presentation tools such as PowerPoint (particularly when used in combination with a digital camera) make excellent use of the verbal, visual, and interpersonal intelligences. There is a nonlinear component to creating a presentation that allows learners to make their own connections between ideas and see new relationships. Similarly, an online collaborative project can reinforce the logical, visual, and kinesthetic elements of the lesson while adding to its interpersonal and intrapersonal dimensions. Such a project could also be used to bring in the musical and existential intelligences, if that is appropriate for your students. In summary, there's no one right answer—it's up to you to determine the most effective focus for your lesson!

By the time you complete this POMAT process, you will be surprised at how much clearer you can see your choices. No, it's not prepackaged and ready to fly, and there's no one right answer. You have to carefully consider the context for the lesson to determine the answer that's right for you. You can decide:

- not to use digital technologies to keep the lesson finite and circumscribed.

- to add nontechnological tasks to the lesson to stimulate additional intelligences. These might include an oral presentation, a challenge to identify patterns in bridge design, or a discussion of bridge aesthetics and the effect of bridges on the environment.

- to use probeware or Excel to enhance the lesson objective.

- to use PowerPoint to extend the lesson without changing its primary focus.

- to choose an online collaborative project and develop a unit that will take the lesson in a completely new direction that opens it up to a variety of intelligences.

Practical Examples

In addition to mapping out a lesson using the POMAT approach, you should examine the balance of intelligences in your plan using the Wheel of MI Domains (see chapter 2). Consider Mrs. Betteridge's favorite kindergarten lesson on sinking and floating. For years, she has used a lesson that employs a large tub of water and all kinds of materials children can experiment with. To find out which intelligences are being stimulated by this lesson, Mrs. Betteridge first considers her objectives:

Objectives

1 The learner will predict with at least 75% success whether a given material will sink or float.

2 The learner will sort the materials into two groups: sinking and floating.

She looks at the Wheel of MI Domains and quickly identifies objective 1 as addressing the logical intelligence. After much thought she decides that objective 2 is addressing both the musical and naturalist intelligences. In short, she has a highly analytic lesson. Is there anything wrong with having a highly analytic lesson? Not at all! However, if Mrs. Betteridge wants to expand the scope of this lesson to stimulate additional intelligences, she can return to the Wheel of MI Domains to consider the best way to integrate other intelligences. After further consideration, Mrs. Betteridge determines that, while there is already a kinesthetic component to the activity, she would like to strengthen it by having the students weigh each material before testing their hypothesis. They can use this information in forming their hypothesis, and they can sort materials not only by sinking and floating but also by weight. She also wants the children to use their visual intelligence to create a diagram that displays their findings with drawings of each material. She rewrites her objectives accordingly:

Objectives

1 The learner will weigh with at least 80% accuracy each material in both a dry and wet state. (Kinesthetic, Logical)

2 The learner will predict with at least 75% success whether a given material will sink or float. (Musical, Logical)

3 The learner will sort the materials into four groups: sinking, floating, dry weight, and wet weight. (Naturalist)

4 Using picture symbols, the learner will create a diagram that reflects the information gathered from the experiment. (Visual)

Now Mrs. Betteridge is ready to tighten up her lesson and successfully address five of the nine intelligences. Used in this way, the Wheel of MI Domains can be extremely helpful in balancing existing lessons.

Table 16 shows how Leigh Anne Rogers made her second-grade dinosaur unit come alive by considering MI theory and the uses of technology.

Integrated Dinosaur Research Unit

(Continued)

MATERIALS	INTELLIGENCES
Videos *Eyewitness Dinosaur* (Lionheart Television) *Death of the Dinosaur* (Turner Home Entertainment)	Verbal Visual Musical

PROCEDURE

Preparation
- Run materials for dinosaur sort (AIMS).
- Purchase gummy dinosaurs for sort.
- Gather materials.
- Contact Children's Museum of Kansas City to schedule a visit with the Classroom on Wheels. (This is a mobile classroom with a themed lesson on excavating fossils. It's like a field trip that visits you!)
- Search the Internet and bookmark appropriate sites for student use.
- Schedule library research time.
- Send notes home to parents about food needed for the culminating activity.
- Organize centers: create a listening center with dinosaur books, an Internet center on a networked computer, an art center for drawing and coloring dinosaurs, a poetry center with dinosaur poetry, and a math center with measurement and graphing activities.

Activities

Day 1
- Students complete a web about dinosaurs in the computer lab using Inspiration software, adding all the information they already know.
- After returning to the classroom, students make a web containing information compiled by the class. Students also record any questions they have.
- Read *Giant Dinosaurs* together and complete a comprehension activity. Measure some of the actual giant lengths within the school building.

Intelligences for Day 1: Verbal, Logical, Visual, Naturalist, Existential

Day 2
- Explore Web sites as a class, then make sites available as a center choice.
- In small groups, students read various Bernard Most titles and work together on comprehension activities.

Intelligences for Day 2: Verbal, Logical, Visual, Intrapersonal, Interpersonal, Existential

Day 3
- Small groups continue to read various Bernard Most titles.
- The teacher reads *If the Dinosaurs Came Back* aloud to the class. Students create a classroom mural following the artist's style in the book illustrations.

Intelligences for Day 3: Verbal

Day 4
- Read *Digging for Dinosaurs* aloud as a class. Explore fossil collections that were brought to class to share by the teacher and students.

Intelligences for Day 4: Visual, Kinesthetic, Intrapersonal, Interpersonal, Existential

(Continued)

Integrated Dinosaur Research Unit

(Continued)

PROCEDURE	INTELLIGENCES
Day 5 • Visit Classroom on Wheels for an excavation activity. Have students participate in the dinosaur sort and fossil-finding grid activity.	Verbal Logical Visual Interpersonal Naturalist
Day 6 • Begin reading *Cam Jansen and the Mystery of the Dinosaur Bones*.	Logical Visual Interpersonal Naturalist Existential
Day 7 • Continue reading *Cam Jansen*. • Have the students begin researching a class dinosaur: Compsagnathus.	Verbal
Day 8 • Read *The Magic School Bus in the Time of the Dinosaurs* together as a class. Learn about time periods and Pangea. • Have students continue research of the class dinosaur and share any information found. Begin planning for the class presentation of the material.	Verbal Logical
Day 9 • Have students complete the presentation and practice it. • Watch a selected dinosaur video.	Verbal Logical Interpersonal Existential
Day 10 • Unit culmination! The class gathers in the library to share material about the dinosaurs with other classes. • Have an Herbivore, Carnivore, Omnivore Feast.	Verbal Logical Visual Musical Interpersonal
Follow-Up Provide opportunities for extending learning through independent studies about other dinosaurs.	Verbal Logical Visual Musical Kinesthetic Interpersonal Existential

PRODUCT	
Student dinosaur presentations.	Verbal Visual Logical Musical Interpersonal Naturalist

(Continued)

Integrated Dinosaur Research Unit

(Continued)

ASSESSMENT	INTELLIGENCES
Students will be evaluated on the following:	
• Research gathered on class dinosaur.	Verbal Logical
• Comprehension activities from selected readings.	Verbal Logical
• Completed web of student learning about dinosaurs.	Verbal Logical Visual Kinesthetic Intrapersonal Naturalist
• Log of Web sites visited during center times and other completed center materials.	Visual Logical Naturalist
• Class participation.	Interpersonal

Table 17 shows how Leigh Anne's unit looks in a POMAT chart. Note how explicitly Leigh Anne incorporates all nine intelligences in this lesson plan. Each intelligence is stimulated by one or more of the procedures, and seven of nine are similarly targeted by the lesson's objectives, materials, and assessment. It's possible that Leigh Anne could come up with additional ways to address the intrapersonal or interpersonal intelligences through her selection of technologies, but this is already a well-distributed accommodation of multiple intelligences!

TABLE 17

Integrated Dinosaur Research Unit POMAT Table

INTELLIGENCES	POMAT				
	Procedure	*Objective*	*Materials*	*Assessment*	*Technology*
Verbal	✔	✔	✔	✔	✔
Logical	✔	✔	✔	✔	✔
Visual	✔	✔	✔	✔	✔
Kinesthetic	✔	✔	✔	✔	✔
Musical	✔	✔	✔	✔	✔
Interpersonal	✔	✔	✔	✔	
Intrapersonal	✔				
Naturalist	✔	✔	✔	✔	✔
Existential	✔				
NOTES	KWL charts, reading, excavating, researching, synthesizing information, celebrating learning with other classes	Scientific method, explaining earth's geology, measurement and directed reading and listening activities	Literature, poetry, video, measuring tools, excavation materials	Class research, class webs, comprehension activities, completed center materials	Literature, computer, television, video, excavation tools, Inspiration, Excel, Microsoft Internet Explorer

Resources for Further Study

Print

Brewer, T. (2003). *Technology integration in the 21st century classroom.* Eugene, OR: Visions Technology.

Johnson, D. L., Maddux, C. D., & Liu, L. (2000). *Integration of technology into the classroom: Case studies.* Binghamton, NY: Haworth Press.

Moersch, C. (2002). *Beyond hardware: Using existing technology to promote higher-level thinking.* Eugene, OR: International Society for Technology in Education.

Moursund, D. (2002). *Project-based learning using information technology* (2nd ed.). Eugene, OR: International Society for Technology in Education.

NETS Project. (2000). *National educational technology standards for students: Connecting curriculum and technology*. Eugene, OR: International Society for Technology in Education.

Price, K. M., & Nelson, K. L. (2002). *Daily planning for today's classroom: A guide to writing lesson and activity plans*. Florence, KY: Wadsworth.

Rief, S. F., & Heimburge, J. A. (2002). *How to reach and teach all students in the inclusive classroom: Ready-to-use strategies, lessons and activities teaching students with diverse learning needs*. Hoboken, NJ: Jossey-Bass.

Online

Aligning and Articulating Standards Across the Mathematics Curriculum:
www.ncrel.org/sdrs/areas/issues/content/cntareas/math/ma400.htm

Curriculum Mapping:
http://currmap.ncrel.org/default.htm

Multiple Intelligence Lesson Plans:
www.uwsp.edu/education/lwilson/lessons/MI/miindex.htm

Social Studies Multiple Intelligence Lesson Plan:
www.bsu.edu/classes/cantu/philippondominiclessonplan.htm

Using Technology to Differentiate Instruction:
www.lakelandschools.org/EDTECH/Differentiation/home.htm

What Is a Matter of Understanding?:
www.ascd.org/publications/books/198199/chapter2.html

What Is Backward Design?:
www.pgcps.pg.k12.md.us/~croom/what_is_backward_design.htm

Reflections

1 Can intelligences influence your instructional approach just as they influence student approaches to learning?

2 Which intelligences are easiest for you to accommodate in your classroom? Why?

3 Which technologies do you use most frequently? Which intelligences do they best accommodate?

4 How can the POMAT method help you maximize the potential of existing lessons for incorporating multiple intelligences and technology?

7

Building
New Instruction

H aving worked through existing lessons, you now have a good frame of reference for developing MI lessons from scratch. From our previous work we know that:

- A lesson cannot be expected to successfully incorporate all nine intelligences at once. To accommodate an intelligence, a lesson or activity should utilize that intelligence for the explicit purpose of instruction.

- The objective comes first, the targeted intelligences come second, and the selected technologies (if any) come third when building a lesson plan.

- The assessment task should have a direct connection to the stated objective and should utilize the same intelligences stimulated by the lesson's activities.

- The Wheel of MI Domains can be used to check and balance the intelligences addressed in a lesson.

In this chapter, we will apply what we've learned to build new instruction that engages multiple intelligences.

Brainstorming Possibilities

The first step in developing a brand new MI lesson or unit is to brainstorm ideas for making connections across the intelligences. This can be especially fruitful when a team of teachers works together, creating a dynamic in which each suggestion stimulates further thinking and the generation of additional possibilities. Start by placing the lesson topic or unit theme in the middle of a page and arranging each of the nine intelligences around its periphery. Focusing on one intelligence at a time, come up with as many instructional ideas as you can that relate to your topic. At this point, there is no need to give detailed descriptions. The best brainstorming sessions are "lightning rounds" in which ideas are rattled off without hesitation. There will be time later to decide which of these ideas warrant further consideration.

One digital tool that works well for generating ideas is Inspiration. This concept-mapping tool allows you to set up a main idea and then generate additional ideas around it (Figure 7). Its "rapid fire" feature allows you to add ideas and links by simply hitting the Enter key each time you come up with something new. Inspiration also provides for easy manipulation of each map item, so you can rearrange items and show visual connections to related ideas.

FIGURE 7
Example of an Inspiration Concept Map

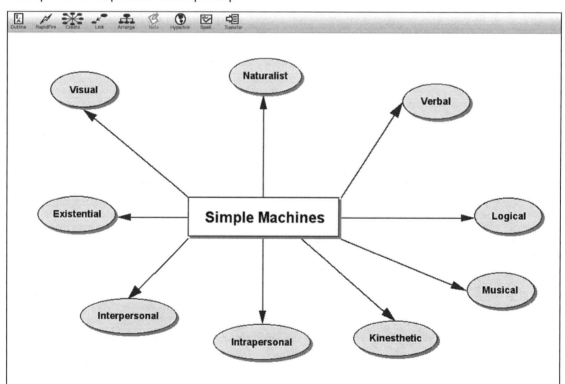

Once you have generated a variety of ideas, you have the luxury of picking and choosing the activities that will most benefit your lesson or unit. For a single lesson, select activities that stimulate three to five intelligences. For a larger unit, select activities that will stimulate all nine intelligences. With these activities selected, you are now ready to write your lesson or unit plan.

An MI Lesson Template

Table 18 presents a lesson template that incorporates MI and technology. It includes all the key components of a standard lesson, while encouraging the alignment of the objective with the particular intelligences and technologies that are to be used. There is a column for indicating standards (such as ISTE's NETS for Students, subject standards, or your state learning standards), and space in the Materials and Procedure sections for identifying intelligences. A Reflection section allows for specific evaluation of the technology employed with regard to the intelligences and the lesson objective.

TABLE 18

Multiple Intelligences Lesson Template

LESSON TITLE:
TEACHER:
GRADE LEVEL:
SUBJECT(S):   TIME FRAME:

OBJECTIVE(S)	INTELLIGENCES	TECHNOLOGIES	STANDARDS
			(NETS, subject, and state standards)

MATERIALS	INTELLIGENCES
PROCEDURE	
PRODUCT	
ASSESSMENT	

REFLECTION

How did the technologies used accommodate the intelligences you identified?

If the technologies used were not effective, what can you recommend as an alternative application to use with this lesson the next time it is taught?

How did the intelligences identified improve student mastery of the objective or objectives?

Did you observe other intelligences come into play during the lesson? What were they and how did they aid in student learning?

Which other intelligences could be included in this lesson? How might they be incorporated?

With this flexible template, you can adjust the size of different sections to meet your planning needs. Also, the tabular format of the Objective section allows for a quick visual scan of the intelligences addressed and their alignment with the objective and technologies. Note that the right-hand column below the Standards section is for listing intelligences as you identify their use. This promotes checking the actual use of intelligences in the Materials, Procedure, Product, and Assessment sections with those stated in the Objective. The Reflection section asks the teacher to evaluate whether the prescribed technologies did indeed stimulate the intended intelligences by focusing on specific observations and outcomes from the lesson. If the technologies used did not meet expectations, the teacher is asked to suggest other technologies that may be more appropriate when the lesson is taught again. Additionally, the Reflection section asks the teacher to evaluate how stimulation of the targeted intelligences promoted student learning as defined by the objective, and whether other intelligences also came into play. This provides valuable insight for the teacher the next time the lesson is implemented in the classroom.

Let's look at an example of an MI lesson. Mr. Martineau is planning a lesson on spreadsheets for his seventh graders. It is an introductory lesson, but he's not sure how best to introduce this sophisticated productivity tool. He takes a look at the Wheel of MI Domains and determines that an introductory lesson on spreadsheets will have to focus on the logical intelligence as a point of student orientation. Mr. Martineau identifies the logical intelligence in the analytic domain, and then seeks to find an intelligence in the interactive and introspective domains to balance the logical approach. He determines that the visual and kinesthetic intelligences in the introspective domain and the verbal intelligence in the interactive domain will provide a nice balance for his lesson. Mr. Martineau brainstorms activities specifically for these three intelligences and then identifies the learning objectives for these activities, thereby mapping the objectives to the intelligences.

Objectives

1 The learner will identify, with at least 75% accuracy, a cell, a range of cells, and an auto sum formula by using row and column coordinates. (Logical)

2 The learner will, with at least 80% success, use index cards to visually create a spreadsheet of four columns and five rows. (Visual, Kinesthetic)

3 The learner will describe, with at least 80% mastery, how a spreadsheet uses a formula to complete a simple computation given a range of cells. (Verbal)

Now Mr. Martineau is ready to proceed with the planning of materials, procedure, product, and assessment. By mapping the intelligences to the objectives as a first step, the teacher ensures that the lesson will be well grounded and will stimulate several different intelligences in the process. Table 19 demonstrates this point.

TABLE 19

Introduction to Spreadsheets Lesson

LESSON TITLE: Introduction to Spreadsheets
TEACHER: Martineau
GRADE LEVEL: 7
SUBJECT(S):   Math   TIME FRAME: 50 minutes

OBJECTIVE(S)	INTELLIGENCES	TECHNOLOGIES	STANDARDS
• The learner will identify, with at least 75% accuracy, a cell, a range of cells, and an auto sum formula by using row and column coordinates.	Logical	Microsoft Excel	**NETS for Students:** **1. Basic operations and concepts** • Students demonstrate a sound understanding of the nature and operation of technology systems.
• The learner will, with at least 80% success, use index cards to visually create a spreadsheet of four columns and five rows.	Visual Kinesthetic		**3. Technology productivity tools** • Students use technology tools to enhance learning, increase productivity, and promote creativity.
• The learner will describe, with at least 80% mastery, how a spreadsheet uses a formula to complete a simple computation, given a range of cells.	Verbal		

MATERIALS	INTELLIGENCES
Index cards Pencils, paper Microsoft Excel	Visual Kinesthetic Logical

PROCEDURE	
Give all students 20 index cards to work with at their desks. • Have students label the cards A1–D5. • Have students organize the cards on their desks by rows (1–5) and columns (A–D). • Lead the class in this exercise on the board at the front of the room and answer any questions.	Visual Kinesthetic Logical
Turn on an LCD projection of a blank Excel spreadsheet. • Have students compare index cards with cells in the spreadsheet. • Practice with the class identifying cells by their coordinates.	Visual Logical
Have students turn on their computers. • Direct students to launch Excel. • Have students click on cells and ranges of cells as you call them out.	Logical

(Continued)

Introduction to Spreadsheets Lesson

(Continued)

PROCEDURE	INTELLIGENCES
Type a series of numbers in columns A–D, rows 1–5. • Have students type a series of numbers into their individual spreadsheets.	Logical
Highlight column A, rows 1–5, and demonstrate the use of the auto sum button on the toolbar to total the series of numbers for that column. • Have students highlight column A on their spreadsheets and use the auto sum function to complete the addition of the series of numbers. • Compare student totals with the teacher's total for column A. • Select the cell that contains the sum for column A and examine the formula bar; discuss how the formula =sum(A1,A5) tells the spreadsheet the function to complete.	Verbal Logical
Have students complete columns B–D in the same way. • Ask students to explain the process for finding the sum of a series of numbers in a spreadsheet, using the terms *cell, range, toolbar, button, highlight, auto sum,* and *formula.*	Verbal Logical
Turn off computers. • Pass out a sheet of blank paper to each student. • Have students diagram and label a spreadsheet that adds up a sum of five numbers using the auto sum function. Collect sheets for evaluation.	Logical

PRODUCT	
Students complete spreadsheet diagrams for evaluation.	Logical Verbal

ASSESSMENT	
Students identify, with 80% accuracy, cell coordinates using index cards.	Visual Kinesthetic
Students identify spreadsheet coordinates and use the auto sum feature correctly three out of four times.	Logical
Learners explain the process of using the auto sum function for finding the sum of a series of numbers with correct terminology at least four out of five times.	Verbal Logical

REFLECTION

How did the technologies used accommodate the intelligences you intended?
Excel strongly reinforced the logical intelligence by providing a structure for lining up numbers and creating an elementary formula.

If the technologies used were not effective, can you recommend an alternative application to use with this lesson the next time it is taught?
The technologies used were effective.

(Continued)

Introduction to Spreadsheets Lesson

(Continued)

REFLECTION

How did the intelligences identified improve student mastery of the objective or objectives?
Students who do not usually do well on logical tasks were able to see the format of a spreadsheet. The verbal components helped students to internalize and express their understanding of the spreadsheet algorithm.

Did you observe other intelligences come into play during the lesson? What were they and how did they aid in student learning?
Yes. The musical intelligence came into play as students recognized a repeated pattern in adding each column. Comparing formulas for each column also aided in understanding of the spreadsheet auto sum function.

Which other intelligences could be included in this lesson? How might they be incorporated?
Intrapersonal. Evaluating others' explanations of spreadsheet functions.
Interpersonal. Group work constructing spreadsheets.

Table 20 provides a second example. Ms. Godwin is going to teach her students research skills using digital multimedia resources. Notice how she stimulates a variety of intelligences to make this lesson the most effective it can be.

TABLE 20

Information Skills Lesson

LESSON TITLE: Information Skills

TEACHER: Sherri Godwin, East Clayton Elementary School, Clayton, North Carolina

GRADE LEVEL: 3–4

SUBJECT(S): Language Arts **TIME FRAME:** 1 hour, 15 minutes

OBJECTIVE(S)	INTELLIGENCES	TECHNOLOGIES	STANDARDS
• Students will learn to use multimedia to access information for recreational and informational purposes.	Verbal Logical	Library information system	**NETS for Students:** **1. Basic operations and concepts** • Students are proficient in the use of technology.
• Students will search for information using Grolier's Multimedia Encyclopedia.	Visual Musical	CD-ROM	**2. Social, ethical, and human issues** • Students practice responsible use of technology systems, information, and software.
• Students will listen to and interact with multimedia by using Living Books.	Visual Musical	CD-ROM	
• Students will use Internet resources available through www.yahooligans.com.	Verbal Naturalist	Browser	**5. Technology research tools** • Students use technology to locate, evaluate, and collect information from a variety of sources.

MATERIALS	INTELLIGENCES
Printouts of digital sources	Verbal
Art supplies	Visual

(Continued)

Information Skills Lesson

(Continued)

PROCEDURE	INTELLIGENCES
Working in groups of two, students will complete the following tasks:	Interpersonal

Task 1: Grolier's Multimedia Encyclopedia (GME)
• Students will click on the GME icon.
• Students will choose one of the following topics:
   Dog
   Library
   Lindbergh's Transatlantic Flight
   North Carolina Facts About
   Symphony
• Students will visit the Related Media and Sound sections.
• Students will click on links related to pictures or sounds.
• Students will enlarge pictures.
• Students will listen to sounds.
• Students will save and print information they wish to share.
	Intrapersonal
	
	Visual
	Musical

Task 2: Living Books
• Students will choose one of the following:
   Arthur's Computer Adventure
   The Cat in the Hat
   Just Grandma and Me
   Shelia Rae, the Brave
   The Tortoise and the Hare
• Students will complete the activities associated with one of the Living Books. Some activities will be completed away from the computer with writing or art supplies.
• Students will save and print their work.
	Intrapersonal
	
	Verbal
	Visual
	Musical

Task 3: Yahooligans • Students will access the Internet and type in www.yahooligans.com. • Students will find the School Bell heading and click on the Language Arts link. • Students will scroll down to Word Games. • Students will click on Hangman. • Students will play several rounds of Hangman to test their wits. • Students will scroll down to Wacky Web Tales and create stories. • Students will save and print their stories.	Naturalist Verbal
PRODUCT	
By the end of this lesson, students will have a hard copy of three completed activities.	Visual Verbal Logical Naturalist
ASSESSMENT	
Students will have a collection of materials in hard copy from three digital sources.	Visual
Students will be able to describe the steps for accessing each source by referencing the printouts they have from the lesson.	Verbal Logical
Students will be able to classify printouts from each source based on the information on the printouts from the lesson.	Naturalist

(Continued)

Information Skills Lesson

(Continued)

REFLECTION

How did the technologies used accommodate the intelligences you identified?
The digital resources stimulated the verbal, logical, visual, musical, and naturalist intelligences.

If the technologies used were not effective, can you recommend as an alternative application to use with this lesson the next time it is taught?
The technologies used were effective.

How did the intelligences identified improve student mastery of the objective or objectives?
They especially provided the opportunity for students to complete an activity using each resource and printing out a finished product. This allowed extended time for stimulating the nontraditional visual and musical intelligences for research.

Did you observe other intelligences come into play during the lesson? What were they and how did they aid in student learning?
Yes. The kinesthetic intelligence came into play as students completed art activities related to the Living Books.

Which other intelligences could be included in this lesson? How might they be incorporated?
Existential. Have students locate and respond to works of art.

By brainstorming possibilities for the different intelligences and then using the MI lesson template, teachers can easily tie together objectives, intelligences, and technologies from lesson to lesson.

An MI Unit Template

MI-inspired units of instruction can be developed in the same way as these individual lessons. Rather than brainstorming activities for specific objectives, though, you generate ideas for unit goals. The template for mapping goals to intelligences and technologies looks like Table 21.

TABLE 21

Multiple Intelligences Unit Template

UNIT TITLE:
TEACHER:
GRADE LEVEL:
SUBJECT(S):   TIME FRAME:

GOALS	INTELLIGENCES	TECHNOLOGIES	STANDARDS
			(NETS, subject, and state standards)

MATERIALS	INTELLIGENCES
PROCEDURE	
PRODUCT	
ASSESSMENT	

Table 22 shows how Ms. English employed this template to develop an elections unit using technology and the intelligences.

TABLE 22

Presidential Elections Unit

UNIT TITLE: Presidential Elections
TEACHER: Betty Jo English, The Pruden Center for Industry and Technology, Suffolk, Virginia
GRADE LEVEL: 9
SUBJECT(S): Computer Applications, Social Studies   TIME FRAME: 6 weeks

GOALS	INTELLIGENCES	TECHNOLOGIES	STANDARDS
• To use graphic software to create or manipulate graphics or pictures.	Visual Kinesthetic	Draw	NETS for Students: 1. Basic operations and concepts • Students are
• To reinforce knowledge of United States geography.	Existential	Text WWW CD-ROM	proficient in the use of technology.
• To use electronic spreadsheet software to record and analyze data through graphs.	Logical Visual Musical	Excel	2. Social, ethical, and human issues • Students develop positive attitudes toward technology
• To use database software to create a voter registration record, file, and report.	Verbal Logical Naturalist	Access	uses that support lifelong learning, collaboration, personal pursuits, and productivity.
• To use desktop publishing techniques to create a variety of documents.	Verbal Visual	Publisher	3. Technology productivity tools • Students use technology tools to
• To use various research techniques.	Verbal Logical	WWW CD-ROM	enhance learning, increase productivity, and promote creativity.
• To increase knowledge of the election process for the president of the United States.	Logical Intrapersonal Interpersonal	WWW CD-ROM Videotape	• Students use productivity tools to collaborate in constructing technology-enhanced models, preparing publications, and producing other creative works.

(Continued)

Presidential Elections Unit

(Continued)

GOALS	INTELLIGENCES	TECHNOLOGIES	STANDARDS
			4. Technology communication tools • Students use a variety of media and formats to communicate information and ideas effectively to multiple audiences. **5. Technology research tools** • Students use technology to locate, evaluate, and collect information from a variety of sources. **6. Technology problem-solving and decision-making tools** • Students use technology resources for solving problems and making informed decisions.

MATERIALS	INTELLIGENCES
Voter registration form	Interpersonal
Sample presidential ballot	Intrapersonal
Legal-size printer paper	Visual
Masking tape	Kinesthetic
Audio tape	Musical
Brochure paper	Visual
Hardware Networked computers with Internet connection	Existential
Color printers	Visual
Digital camera	Visual
Scanner	Visual
Audio tape recorder	Musical

(Continued)

Presidential Elections Unit

(Continued)

MATERIALS	INTELLIGENCES
Software	
Desktop publishing software	Verbal Visual
Electronic spreadsheet software	Logical Visual
Desktop presentation software	Logical Naturalist
Graphic/draw software	Visual Kinesthetic
HTML editor	Visual Kinesthetic
Internet browser	Visual Interpersonal
Web Sites	
Web White & Blue: www.webwhiteblue.org	Intrapersonal
By the People: Election 2004: www.pbs.org/elections/kids/educators.html	Existential
The Center for Responsive Politics: www.opensecrets.org/presidential/index.asp	Intrapersonal
ABC News Politics: http://abcnews.go.com/sections/politics/	Existential
Vote Net: www.votenet.com	Interpersonal
CNN Election News: http://cnn.com/ELECTION/2004/	Existential
Washington Post Election Coverage: www.washingtonpost.com/wpdyn/politics/elections/2004/	Existential
Project Vote Smart: www.vote-smart.org	Intrapersonal
Project Vote Smart Youth Inclusion: www.vote-smart.org/yip/	Intrapersonal
C-SPAN Election 2004: www3.capwiz.com/c-span/e4/	Existential
U.S. Electoral College Home Page: www.nara.gov/fedreg/ec-hmpge.html	Logical Musical
The Gallup Poll: www.gallup.com/index.html	Interpersonal
Video Resources	
PBS series *The American President*	Logical Musical
C-SPAN current activities programming	Verbal Visual
Videotaped campaign ads	Verbal Visual

(Continued)

Presidential Elections Unit

(Continued)

PROCEDURE	INTELLIGENCES
Preparation Hold a group discussion of steps taken in selecting a president, including the role of primaries, conventions, polls, and debates.	Verbal Interpersonal Intrapersonal Existential
Activities *1 Steps in Selecting a President* • After a whole-class discussion of the steps and small-group research on the Internet about primaries and conventions, students will work in groups of two using desktop publishing or graphic software to create a flowchart of the steps or a graphic of the campaign trail.	Logical Interpersonal Visual
2 Political Vocabulary • Give students a list of political vocabulary words. Working in small groups, the students will use various research materials to locate appropriate definitions for each word. • Students will use desktop publishing software to create a crossword puzzle using their definitions. Puzzles will be printed and shared with U.S. government teachers for classroom use.	Verbal Logical
3 Registering to Vote • Invite the local voter registrar as a guest speaker to discuss who may register to vote and methods of voter registration in your state. • After reviewing actual voter registration forms, students will use desktop publishing software to create a mock voter registration form for use in the schoolwide election. • Students will work in small groups to visit each classroom to have students register for the mock election. • Using database software, create a database of registered voters for the mock election. Create a report for use on Election Day to verify voter registration.	Verbal Logical Interpersonal Naturalist Existential
4 Who Are the Candidates? • In small groups, students will use the Internet to research the main candidates for U.S. president and vice president. • Students will use research results to create a candidate biography in one of the following modes: (a) desktop presentation, (b) Web page, (c) brochure, or (d) newsletter.	Verbal Visual
5 What Are the Issues? • Students will bring in news articles on a weekly basis covering the issues and the candidates' views or positions. Conduct a whole-class oral discussion of the articles. Display the articles in the classroom for reference. • Have students work in small groups to develop the layout for a comparison table, chart, or grid on the candidates' views on at least eight major issues. • Have students use appropriate software to generate the comparison table, chart, or grid.	Verbal Intrapersonal Interpersonal Naturalist Existential
6 Candidates on the Road • Students will be divided into teams by party. Each team will use the newspaper, television news, or Internet for a daily check of where the candidates for their party are campaigning. Using a U.S. map and graphics software, students will plot the movements of the candidates during the campaign. • Hold a class discussion concerning why some states have more campaigning activity. Have students discuss why they think that candidates are campaigning more in these states.	Verbal Logical Visual Intrapersonal Interpersonal

(Continued)

Presidential Elections Unit

(Continued)

PROCEDURE	INTELLIGENCES
7 Campaign Ads • The whole class will view videos of various campaign ads. Conduct a class discussion of the effects of negative ads. • Have students use desktop publishing software to create campaign posters for candidates. Use posters in hallways for the mock election. *Or:* Have students write and record a radio campaign ad. *Or:* Have students write and use desktop presentation software to create a television campaign ad.	Verbal Visual Musical Intrapersonal Interpersonal
8 The Ballot • After reviewing a sample presidential ballot, students will use desktop publishing software to create election ballots for the schoolwide mock election. • The class will vote for the ballot to be used for the election. • Use a copying machine to produce enough ballots for the number of registered voters.	Visual Intrapersonal Kinesthetic
9 The Electoral College • Working in small groups, students will use the Internet or other current reference sources to determine the number of electoral votes for each state. • Students will use electronic spreadsheet software to create a spreadsheet listing each state and the number of electoral votes. This spreadsheet will be saved to use after the actual election.	Logical Naturalist
10 Stage a Mock Election • The class will designate each class as a specific state for Electoral College purposes. Students will modify their Electoral College spreadsheet with this information. • On Election Day, students will go to each class, check the registration database report to verify the student has registered to vote, distribute a ballot, and have students return their ballots to the ballot box. • The class will count the ballots by class. A student recorder will draw a graph on the chalkboard and record results by class. Students will then modify their Electoral College spreadsheet showing popular vote by class (state). • Using the Electoral College spreadsheet, students will add columns for each candidate to record the allocation of electoral votes received. This data will be used to create a pie chart displaying Electoral College results.	Logical Visual Interpersonal Existential
11 After the Vote • The day after the election, students will create another electronic spreadsheet using the Electoral College data. Students will use the morning newspaper or the Internet to record the national election results. The class will create a pie chart of the results. • Students will compare the mock election results with the actual election results. Conduct a class discussion of how these compare and why.	Verbal Logical Visual Musical Naturalist Existential
Follow-Up Hold a group discussion of the election results. Analyze why the students think voters made their decisions. What became the major issue of the campaign?	Verbal Logical Visual Musical Intrapersonal Interpersonal Naturalist Existential

(Continued)

Presidential Elections Unit	

(Continued)

PRODUCT	INTELLIGENCES
Students will create a product for each activity. 1. Flowchart of steps in selecting a president 2. Crossword puzzle of political terms 3. Mock voter registration form and database of registered voters 4. Candidate biography 5. Issue comparison piece 6. Class discussion on campaign movements (evaluate class participation) 7. Campaign ads 8. Election ballots 9. Electoral vote spreadsheet 10. Mock election spreadsheet 11. Analysis of mock election and actual election.	Verbal Logical Visual Musical Kinesthetic Intrapersonal Interpersonal Naturalist Existential

ASSESSMENT	
Students will be asked to organize each product created during the unit within a unit portfolio. Students will be graded using a rubric.	Verbal Logical Visual Musical Kinesthetic Intrapersonal Interpersonal Naturalist Existential

Choosing to integrate multiple intelligences and technology into this study unit expands the possibilities for students because they are not only learning about the electoral process, they are actually experiencing it in a variety of ways that makes use of all nine intelligences. You can tell just by reading over Betty Jo's plan that her students will be immersed in a series of learning experiences so meaningful and memorable that they will be easily retained.

Table 23 shows how Carol LaVallee created similar learning connections for her students in a science unit for her students.

TABLE 23

Amazon Rainforest Unit

UNIT TITLE: Amazon Rainforest
TEACHER: Carol LaVallee, Venice Area Middle School, Venice, Florida
GRADE LEVEL: 6
SUBJECT(S): Geography, History, World Cultures, Economics   TIME FRAME: 2 weeks

GOALS	INTELLIGENCES	TECHNOLOGIES	STANDARDS
• Students will describe ways regions are interconnected and interdependent.	Verbal Logical Visual	Video Web page	**NETS for Students:** **3. Technology productivity tools** • Students use technology tools to enhance learning, increase productivity, and promote creativity.
• Students will compare and contrast ways various cultures use similar resources and environments.	Verbal Logical Musical Naturalist Existential	Draw/paint program	
• Students will recognize the environmental consequences resulting from people changing the physical environment.	Verbal Logical Musical Intrapersonal Naturalist Existential	Web site	• Students use productivity tools to collaborate in constructing technology-enhanced models, preparing publications, and producing other creative works.
• Students will describe how various geofeatures have influenced the development and interaction of Latin American cultures.	Verbal Logical Musical Naturalist Existential	Web site	**4. Technology communication tools**
• Students will recognize examples of the arts and architecture that reflect the various cultures in Latin America.	Visual Musical Intrapersonal Naturalist Existential	Web site	• Students use telecommunications to collaborate, publish, and interact with peers, experts, and other audiences.
• Students will describe major characteristics and accomplishments of the Mayan and Aztec civilizations.	Verbal Intrapersonal Existential	Web site	• Students use a variety of media and formats to communicate information and ideas effectively to multiple audiences.
• Students will analyze the effects of European rule in Latin America.	Verbal Logical Intrapersonal Interpersonal Existential	Oral presentation	**5. Technology research tools** • Students use technology to locate, evaluate, and collect information from a variety of sources.
• Students will describe the struggle for independence of Latin American nations.	Verbal Intrapersonal Interpersonal Existential	Oral presentation	

(Continued)

Amazon Rainforest Unit

(Continued)

GOALS	INTELLIGENCES	TECHNOLOGIES	STANDARDS
• Students will describe current issues that affect political, social, and economic systems.	Verbal Intrapersonal Interpersonal Existential	Oral presentation	**5. Technology research tools** • Students evaluate and select new information resources and technological innovations based on the appropriateness to specific tasks.

MATERIALS	INTELLIGENCES
Hardware Computer	Kinesthetic
Digital camera	Visual
Video camera	Visual
Cassette/CD player	Musical
Overhead	Visual
VCR	Visual/Musical
Microphone	Verbal/Musical
Software CD-ROM (encyclopedia, atlas)	Verbal/Logical
Word processor (AppleWorks)	Verbal
Drawing, painting (AppleWorks)	Visual/Kinesthetic
Spreadsheet (AppleWorks)	Logical/Visual
Web page editor (AppleWorks)	Visual/Verbal
Avid Cinema	Visual/Verbal
HyperStudio	Visual/Kinesthetic
Fireworks2 (photo/imaging)	Visual/Kinesthetic
Other Materials Floppy disk	Naturalist
Video cassettes	Visual
Tape cassettes	Musical
Art supplies	Kinesthetic

(Continued)

Amazon Rainforest Unit

(Continued)

PROCEDURE	INTELLIGENCES
Preparation The teacher establishes several stations or centers. Each station is titled with the topic and one of Bloom's taxonomies, for example, Rainforest Knowledge, Rainforest Comprehension, Rainforest Application. At these stations, the teacher supplies instructions for students. Students choose how they are going to present their project and choose their own assessment. Students are given a list of MI-based assessments acceptable to the teacher. Students will choose the assessments they will present to the class, such as a skit, Web page, poster, song, essay, debate, photo essay, or editorial. Students will also make a class rubric with teacher input.	
Activities Students are given a packet of the same instructions found at stations a week before to take home and look over with parents.	Verbal Intrapersonal
Students need to decide which station they will start at. However, students still need to complete all stations. (This way, no one is held back; self-motivators can move ahead while those motivated by the teacher can receive guidance.)	Intrapersonal
At the stations, students will find a task to fulfill. The students choose how to fulfill the tasks at the stations with teacher suggestions of MI activities.	Verbal Logical
Students will then work independently.	
Tasks Reading from a textbook or magazine, writing a journal entry, or recording a journal entry on a cassette.	Verbal
Solving the issue at Ecotourism Game Introduction: www.eduweb.com/ecotourism/eco1.html.	Logical
Watching a movie on the Amazon rainforest and creating a chart or graph depicting rainforest depletion.	Visual Logical Naturalist
Listening to rainforest audioclips at Nature Net: www.naturenet.com.br/eng.htm.	Musical
Making a videotape of students portraying Amazon news reporters, or playing a game on CD-ROM entitled "Amazon Trail."	Interpersonal Intrapersonal
Painting a rainforest image and giving it a name or title.	Kinesthetic Intrapersonal
Making a rainforest plant or animal from construction paper.	Kinesthetic
Conducting research at the ITL Rainforest Lesson Web page: http://scrtec.org/track/tracks/f10668.html.	Verbal Naturalist
Reviewing the Rainforest Alliance Home Page and explaining what is being done today: www.rainforest-alliance.org.	Existential
Follow-Up After all presentations are completed, the teacher will create a quiz on the Internet for students to take at home that evening or at school the next day.	

(Continued)

Amazon Rainforest Unit

(Continued)

PRODUCT	INTELLIGENCES
Presenting a skit, debate, or oral report.	Verbal
Developing a chronology of the growth of a rainforest with related statistics.	Logical
Creating a video, commercial, Web page, poster, or photo essay.	Visual
Developing song lyrics or a music video on rainforest plants.	Musical
Making a painting, clay sculpture, drawing, or model of a rainforest. Cooking using recipes from native rainforest lands.	Kinesthetic
Leading a discussion.	Verbal Interpersonal
Presenting concerns on vanishing rainforests.	Intrapersonal
Presenting rainforest flora and fauna in categories.	Naturalist
Examining the role of rainforests in human survival.	Existential

ASSESSMENT	
At the end of two weeks, students will use the class rubric as they present their projects to the class. The teacher and students in the audience will fill out the rubric during the presentation.	Intrapersonal Interpersonal

Carol first mapped the intelligences to educational standards, and then mapped technologies to specific intelligences in the Materials section. The result is a unit that meets the criteria set forth by the standards and the criteria set forth by the human mind. What student wouldn't want to be part of such a rich, gratifying learning environment as Carol's classroom?

Creating new lessons and units of instruction based on Gardner's theory is a process that requires a good deal of reflection and attention to instructional design. But the reward comes in the high quality of instruction you can provide to your students—learning that will stay with them for a lifetime.

Resources for Further Study

Print

Armstrong, T. (2003). *The multiple intelligences of reading and writing: Making the words come alive.* Alexandria, VA: Association for Supervision and Curriculum Development.

Harris, J. (1998). *Virtual architecture: Designing and directing curriculum-based telecomputing.* Eugene, OR: International Society for Technology in Education.

Hird, A. (2000). *Learning from cyber-savvy students: How Internet-age kids impact classroom teaching.* Sterling, VA: Stylus.

Jacobs, H. H. (1997). *Mapping the big picture: Integrating curriculum and assessment K–12.* Alexandria, VA: Association for Supervision and Curriculum Development.

McKenzie, W. (2004). *Standards-based lessons for tech-savvy students: A multiple intelligences approach.* Worthington, OH: Linworth.

Roberts, P. L., & Kellough, R. D. (2003). *A guide for developing interdisciplinary thematic units* (3rd ed.). Upper Saddle River, NJ: Prentice Hall.

Wiggins, G., & McTighe, J. (1998). *Understanding by design.* Alexandria, VA: Association for Supervision and Curriculum Development.

Online

Education World Lesson Planning Center:
www.education-world.com/a_lesson/

Gateway to Educational Materials:
www.thegateway.org

The George Lucas Educational Foundation:
www.glef.org

Integrating Literature and the Arts into Technology-Based Instruction: A New Unit Model for Educators:
http://surfaquarium.com/new_unit_model.pdf

McREL Lesson Plans:
www.mcrel.org/lesson-plans/index.asp

New York Times Lesson Plan Archive:
www.nytimes.com/learning/teachers/lessons/archive.html

PBS TeacherSource:
http://www.pbs.org/teachersource/

Reflections

1 How do you determine what is a reasonable number of intelligences for a lesson to accommodate?

2 Should a unit of instruction be designed to stimulate all the intelligences? Why or why not?

3 When is it more beneficial to accommodate the intelligences using industrial technologies? When is it more beneficial to use digital technologies? Why do you think so?

4 The two lesson examples in this chapter focus on content, with technology use incidental to the lesson. Other examples have taught technology for technology's sake. Is one approach more valid than the other? Why?

CHAPTER 8

Becoming a
Technoconstructivist

W hen integrating MI theory into instruction, the human variable is perhaps the most important to keep in mind. Many new approaches to instruction have come down the road with great fanfare, only to pass by and disappear over the horizon without causing much of a stir. Ask a veteran teacher what he or she thinks about the latest and greatest innovation in education, and that teacher will likely tell you of similar approaches that were touted and then discarded 15 or 20 years ago. There is rarely anything new under the sun.

So, when something reinvents the fundamental structure of society the way digital technology does, people sit up and take notice. Even if some educators are not thrilled with the idea of having to master these complicated new technologies, they cannot ignore the money being spent on hardware, software, and training—not to mention community expectations—to do just that. In certain states, teacher certification is already being linked to technology proficiency. Reality has hit home as educators choose to either update their training or leave the profession.

Transforming Education

When a new innovation is assimilated into an institution such as public education, it takes on many forces already in place. There are educational reform movements requiring teachers to document and improve the quality of the education children receive. There are pressures from special interest groups that want to emphasize literacy, science, math, social studies, or other areas of the curriculum. Teachers are also preoccupied with doing all they can to promote student success on state standardized achievement tests.

Meanwhile, the educational dollar can stretch only so far. Consequently, priorities are chosen and technology takes its place based on the values and attitudes of local administrators. If you're working in a district where technology is a major emphasis, technology becomes an imperative for all teachers. If you're working in a district where basic skills and core curriculum values are prioritized, technology may not be high on your list of professional priorities.

For the majority of educators who work in a district that has not adopted either extreme, student technology use is determined in individual classrooms, based on the accessibility of technology, the availability of training, and the value a teacher places on technology as an instructional tool. The typical teacher wants to incorporate technology as he or she sees fit. This limits student use of technology to applications that are familiar to that particular teacher.

For example, six fourth-grade classes at school A may be studying the solar system at the same time. Three of the six may have their students creating three-dimensional working models of the relationships among the sun, earth, and moon. One of these three teachers actually bookmarks a short list of excellent Web sites for student research, including a NASA Ask-an-Expert site, sites with pictures taken in space and transmitted to earth, and several sites that use current Web technologies to present interactive animations of the solar system and its phenomena. While the other two teachers are using Styrofoam and papier-mâché to create their models, our technology-connected teacher is asking students to create digital multimedia presentations that will demonstrate working models of the sun, earth, and moon while offering links to vocabulary and external links to Web resources on the subject. These students have expressed interest in creating interactive quizzes at the end of their presentations, and the teacher has already contacted the school Webmaster about posting these finished products on the school site to share with the larger community. Only a small number of children from this entire fourth grade will have the opportunity to study the solar system using digital technology, because only one of the six teachers has made it a priority in her instruction.

Technology not only helps students travel across space, but through time as well. Consider how Faithe Ferrante uses a virtual field trip to immerse students in World War II Europe, shown in Table 24.

TABLE 24

A Virtual Field Trip to WWII Europe Unit

UNIT TITLE: A Virtual Field Trip to WWII Europe

TEACHER: Faithe Ferrante, Long Beach Middle School, Long Beach, New York

GRADE LEVEL: 8

SUBJECT(S): English, Social Studies

TIME FRAME: 5 class periods (42 minutes each) in the computer lab

GOALS	INTELLIGENCES	TECHNOLOGIES	STANDARDS
This assignment allows students to connect to the Holocaust by looking at pictures and reading personal accounts of the events. In this unit, the students visit two locations on virtual field trips: the Anne Frank House (where she hid during the war) and the Auschwitz concentration camp.	Verbal Intrapersonal Existential Visual Interpersonal Naturalist	Computers Internet Microsoft Word Microsoft Powerpoint Browser	**NETS for Students:** **2. Social, ethical, and human issues** • Students understand the ethical, cultural, and societal issues related to technology. • Students practice responsible use of technology systems, information, and software. • Students develop positive attitudes toward technology uses that support lifelong learning, collaboration, personal pursuits, and productivity. **5. Technology research tools** • Students use technology to locate, evaluate, and collect information from a variety of sources. • Students evaluate and select new information resources and technological innovations based on the appropriateness to specific tasks.

(Continued)

A Virtual Field Trip to WWII Europe Unit

(Continued)

MATERIALS	INTELLIGENCES
Anne Frank House and Related Web Sites www.ushmm.org/museum/exhibit/online/hidkid/index/ www.annefrank.com www.library.yale.edu/testimonies www.remember.org	Intrapersonal Visual Existential Verbal
Auschwitz and Related Web Sites http://holocaust-history.org www.holocaustsurvivors.org www.auschwitz-muzeum.oswiecim.pl/html/eng/start/index.php www.wiesenthal.com	Intrapersonal Visual Existential Verbal

PROCEDURE

Preparation The teacher will have provided students with general background information about World War II concentration camps and Anne Frank's life prior to this assignment. The teacher will distribute the assignment during the preparation period and go over it with the class.	Verbal Interpersonal
Activities Students will visit Web sites depicting the secret annex and view pictures of Anne Frank and the other annex members. These experiences will help them better understand Anne's diary. They will also take a virtual field trip to Auschwitz and conduct research on concentration camps.	Visual Verbal Intrapersonal Existential
Anne Frank House Activity While students are visiting the secret annex, have them spend time in the room that Anne shared with Mr. Dussel and answer the following questions: What does the room look like? Does it resemble the room of a typical teenager? Why? Why not? What does the room reveal about Anne's personality? Have students collect one picture artifact from an Anne Frank Web site.	Visual Intrapersonal Existential
Auschwitz Activity Auschwitz was a concentration camp where many victims of the Holocaust wrongfully lost their lives. Have students look at the photo gallery and write a reaction in which they answer the following questions: What would you say to the many people who died at Auschwitz if you had the chance? What have you learned about pain and suffering through their unfortunate experiences? Have students collect three picture artifacts from Auschwitz Web sites.	Visual Verbal Intrapersonal Existential

PRODUCT

Anne Frank House Poster Have students create a digital poster about Anne's experiences in hiding. Students should include pictures and family items, as well as other things that were important to her. They should also include pictures of the secret annex and explanations of what her life was like while she was hiding during the war. Have students include five quotes and citations from Anne's diary on the poster.	Visual Verbal Intrapersonal Existential

(Continued)

A Virtual Field Trip to WWII Europe Unit

(Continued)

PRODUCT	INTELLIGENCES
Auschwitz Journal Ask students to pretend they are Jewish prisoners in Auschwitz during World War II. Have them write five journal entries describing their experiences there. Direct students to use the information they learned during the virtual field trip to create realistic entries.	Verbal Intrapersonal Existential
PowerPoint Presentation Students will show their field trip artifacts to the class in a 3–5 minute oral PowerPoint presentation. During the presentation, students will share their understanding of life in World War II Europe.	Visual Verbal Intrapersonal Existential

ASSESSMENT	
Students will be asked to organize each product created during the unit in a unit portfolio. Students will be graded using a rubric.	Visual Verbal Intrapersonal Existential

Faithe has made a conscious choice about instruction: rather than simply imparting knowledge and training her students to respond correctly when she prompts them for a "right answer," Faithe strives to provide learning experiences that immerse her students in information-rich experiences. During this virtual field trip, her students have the opportunity not only to internalize information about the Holocaust, but to develop their own opinions and ideas based on this experience. As a result, she helps her students develop a much higher mastery of this significant historical event, with a greater ability to demonstrate that understanding on any of a number of assessment tasks.

The key, then, is to choose activities and approaches that encourage critical thinking in students. Force-feeding students with "right answers" may take less time, but does it truly develop mastery? What if the assessment task doesn't test your students in the same way that you've trained them? Are you really teaching them to think, or conditioning them to respond? Many teachers are so sensitive to current trends in accountability and the documentation of student learning that they shy away from using technology to promote critical thinking. "How can we possibly spend a lot of time on computer applications," they wonder, "when there is so much content to cover for state tests that we'll be lucky if these kids are ready in time?" Others who are required to make time for computers in instruction still resist, saying, "All of these higher level applications are fine and dandy, but they aren't going to help my kids fill in the bubbles correctly on standardized tests. What they need is more drill on skills!"

These pressures are very real. In some areas, teachers are actually in danger of losing their jobs if a certain percentage of students do not pass these tests every spring. Each one of us needs to do some soul-searching. Do we sincerely believe that the most effective way to prepare children for standardized tests is to offer instruction that panders to lower levels of thinking?

Jamie's Story

Consider Jamie, a young man I taught in fourth grade just as the Virginia Standards of Learning (SOL) tests were being rolled out statewide. Jamie was functioning below grade level in language arts and mathematics, and he received daily instruction from a specialist in both areas to supplement his regular classwork. Coming from a disadvantaged home, Jamie did not have a lot of the material things other students owned, and even though he lived less than an hour from our nation's capital, he had not been exposed to any of its cultural riches. Jamie's cumulative record sounded all too familiar to this veteran teacher of 14 years. His standardized test scores were extremely low, and his annual report card grades were consistently poor from year to year. Jamie also had regular discipline problems with peers and teachers, as he did not like school.

This was the first year that Virginia schools were expected to have at least 70% of their students pass a state SOL test on Virginia history. All five of us teaching fourth grade in my school felt under the gun to do everything we could to cover 400 years of Virginia history, including economics, government, and current events. As we met to plan at the beginning of the year, three of the teachers were sure that they wanted to focus on social studies: names, dates, places, and map skills, using as many textbooks, worksheets, homework assignments, and quizzes as they could muster. While this was a strongly traditional way to go, I wasn't convinced that our students would be able to master anything more than rote memorization by testing time in May. I knew there had to be other ways to make this mountain of information meaningful for students. A teammate joined me in searching for something just as comprehensive but more supportive of students with different intelligence profiles. We came up with a cache of instructional approaches for the year that the two of us planned to work on together.

That year my students built a wigwam, researched colonial crafts, organized a "colonial day," performed a musical play in the tradition of *1776*, participated in the construction of a Web site on the achievements of Thomas Jefferson, drilled with mop handles over their shoulders in the April mud while singing Civil War songs, used the local newspaper in weekly activities to learn about government and current events, and competed weekly against our rival class in the SOL Olympics (we fondly referred to it as the "SOLympics"), challenging one another in the mastery of Virginia history.

When May rolled around, all five classes took the Virginia SOL Social Studies test. None of the fourth-grade teachers knew how well our kids would test that first year. We all showed deference to one another's methods and supported each other as we waited for the test results to come back. There was a lot of soul-searching on my part during the weeks we waited for the results. What if the drill-and-practice approach worked more successfully? Even worse, what if our highly visible efforts to use more learner-centered approaches to instruction failed and everyone knew it? But it was too late to turn back. The testing was done, the work was turned in, and the chips would fall where they may.

When the test scores came back, the results were riveting. My teammate and I had the only two classes out of the five in which at least 70% of the students passed the test. Granted, both classes scored in the low 70s, but we had gotten over the bar set by the state. This was wonderful validation of our intuition that there had to be a better way to cover such a huge volume of material successfully.

As I looked more closely at each of my student's scores, I was glad to see that almost everyone scored relatively close to my expectations. Even those who didn't pass the test did well enough that I knew they had grown a lot during the year. The evidence clearly indicated that all students gave their very best effort.

Then I came to Jamie's score sheet. I was astounded. Here was a young man struggling to meet the minimum requirements for promotion at each grade level, and he had scored in the 99th percentile on the test! I went over the way the scores broke down for him, and time and time again he had been able to determine the correct answer for each test item. He had outscored every other student in my class!

I thought about this in amazement. How could someone who struggles with reading comprehension do so well on a standardized test? As I looked back over the year, I remembered Jamie's participation in all our Virginia-themed activities. Verbally, he was always able to master the material, and he was quite the ham during our production of a colonial-era play and our weekly SOLympics competitions. He also loved the Civil War drilling, the singing, the class wigwam, and the study of Jefferson.

I spoke with his Chapter 1 teacher to get her take on his success, and she informed me that she was not at all surprised because Jamie had truly blossomed as a reader that year in her room. She had been working with him since kindergarten, and she was amazed at how his attitude toward school and reading had changed. As I put together the big picture of Jamie's year, my amazement subsided and I began to feel humbled by his momentous achievements.

I will never forget the lessons I learned that year. Yes, I had always subscribed to developmentally appropriate practice and multimodal learning. I had always talked a good game and wanted to implement as much of it as I could. But there was always a shadow of doubt in my mind, placed there by colleagues who did not subscribe to such child-centered practices. For me, Jamie's accomplishments were all the validation I needed. I knew now that everything that made sense to me about teaching and learning actually did work. Despite the strong incentives to "drill and kill," the student-centered approaches that we had chosen had won out.

I believe all teachers would be willing to let go of their skills checklists and worksheets if they didn't feel so accountable to state standards. After all, most of us didn't get into teaching for the money. We got into teaching to see that spark in children when they get excited about new learning. That's what it's all about.

A Four-Tier Model

Technology, however, is a different story. Many teachers entered the profession long before the microcomputer appeared in schools. Technology has been thrust upon them as one more requirement they never agreed to when they first entered the classroom. How do teachers respond to the challenge of integrating technology into their existing instructional practices? Scott Noon of Classroom Connect examined this question and came up with a four-tier model of teacher training in technology. Each tier of the model demonstrates an identifiable stage in teacher technology proficiency. The model reflects the way that teachers learn to use technology and the journey they make in the process. Let's take a look at Noon's model (Table 25).

TABLE 25

Noon's Four-Tier Model of Technological Proficiency for Teachers

STAGE	DESCRIPTION	EXAMPLES
Preliterate	Not yet using technology for personal or instructional purposes	Traditional media and materials
Technocrat	Experimenting with technology but unsure of its overall dependability and usefulness	Demonstration station with LCD projector, computer lab, learning station with computer
Technotraditionalist	Using technology proficiently to accomplish traditional classroom tasks	Word processed lesson plans, electronic grade book, e-mail, digital slideshows
Technoconstructivist	Using technology to completely change approaches to teaching and learning in the classroom	Online projects, virtual field trips, WebQuests, digital portfolios, virtual classrooms

The Preliterate User

This is where we all begin. We are aware of technology's presence in our buildings, even in our classrooms, but we do not have the training, experience, or confidence to use the technology. Teachers who fit in this category have yet to establish an e-mail account, use a word processor, or even find a piece of appropriate software that can be used with students to enrich instruction. Perhaps technology seems like another entire body of knowledge that there just isn't time to master. Or perhaps technology seems like a lot of fluff that gets in the way of honest, on-task instructional time.

For each teacher the reasons may vary, but the overwhelming response I hear from educator groups no matter where I go is, "We just haven't had the training we need to make good use of all the hardware and software that's been purchased for us to use." Educational institutions in general are very quick to throw money at a new issue or innovation, and then very quick to move on to other trendy ideas without giving invested initiatives time to fully realize their potential. Many teachers are telling us that this is happening with technology: they don't have the training time or funds needed to complete the technology puzzle. Few teachers are preliterate users by choice; no one wants to be left behind. And since we all start at this point, perhaps that is the impetus that compels us to move forward and become more proficient with technology. Still, how do we move on without the prerequisite training?

The Technocrat

This second tier of Noon's model is a critical point in teacher technology training. Teachers in this category have ventured out to learn how to use an LCD projector connected to a demonstration computer station. They have made the effort to identify instructional applications that students can successfully use in the computer lab. At the high end of this tier, teachers even dabble in new, more advanced applications to invigorate themselves.

The main characteristic of this category, however, is preoccupation with the technical aspects of technology. How do I turn it on? What do I do if the bulb burns out while I'm presenting to my entire class? What if the server is down and I have 25 children unable to complete the online task I had planned? Of course, the only way to answer these questions is to learn from experience. Technology always offers the possibility of glitches and unforeseen mishaps. High-end users understand this and have learned the tricks of the trade, which include having a Plan B handy whenever technology is going to be used.

By giving teachers the time and support they need to grow as technocrats, we are creating an instructional environment in which technology really gets used because teachers are no longer afraid of it. I believe once teachers can see past their initial fears, they will come to recognize how technology can enrich their lives both personally and professionally.

The Technotraditionalist

For teachers in the third tier of Noon's model, technology is seen as an inherently good thing in instruction, which can be used in a variety of ways around the classroom. Teachers at this level often create word processing templates so they can write their lesson plans in an easy-to-use format. Likewise, technotraditionalist teachers use spreadsheets to create seating charts and electronic grade books. The teachers at this level are high-end users, and they make use of technology to complete the same tasks they have traditionally always accomplished as teachers. Is there anything wrong with that? No! It is an important stage in the development of the technology-savvy teacher. Still, if we are using technology only to keep track of lunch counts and type reports to hang on the wall, how far have we really come? Yes it's more efficient to set up a database to make student mailing labels that you can use all year, but you're still holding on to traditional attitudes about instruction.

If technology is going to be a true agent for change in education (and this remains to be seen), educators at all levels are going to have to be willing to ask themselves fundamental questions about why they continue to do things as they always have. Perhaps some of our preconceptions have to do with growing up in the Industrial Age, when many Digital Age possibilities were not yet available. If technology is to offer any hope for solving traditional problems, then we may have to rethink our assumptions and be willing to go beyond traditionalist uses of technology.

The Technoconstructivist

The technoconstructivist is the highest tier in Noon's model. Here, teachers not only integrate technology into traditional views of instruction, but are willing to reshape those views and explore wholly new learning models made possible by technology. For technoconstructivists, technology is not just an instructional tool, it is a way to transform the classroom into a new and vital learning environment for students.

The technoconstructivist classroom makes use of Web resources, electronic mail, online collaborative projects, synchronous Web-based events, virtual field trips, WebQuests, multimedia presentations, virtual classrooms, interactive simulations, and much, much more. As the Internet breaks down the four physical walls of the classroom as well as the traditional boundaries of time, space, and money, students are able to use higher levels of thinking, apply real-world approaches and solutions, and collaborate with experts and other learners from around the world. The result is a learning revolution, in which the teacher becomes a facilitator and guide to all the learning possibilities in the world around us, virtual and otherwise. The technoconstructivist is the highest level of technological proficiency for teachers, and one we must all aspire to if we are to realize educational technology's full potential.

If we believe that technology is just another tool for instruction, then it is worth no more than any other piece of equipment in our classrooms. When we are willing to let go of our preconceived notions and traditional ideas, however, we can see technology's true potential to transform instruction. As long as we force technology into the Industrial Age model of education, we are limiting its promise. That is why we have not yet seen much research evidence to support the role of technology in instruction. We need to allow technology to transform our classrooms for the Information Age. It cannot do so if it is just superimposed upon a model of teaching that faded with the end of the last century.

Now consider MI theory in light of Noon's model. How does a teacher use MI with technology in any of the first three tiers? One can argue, perhaps, that teachers at the technotraditionalist level are capable of at least accommodating several intelligences at once, maybe without even realizing it. My question is: "Is this what we really want for good instruction: chancing on effective strategies without even realizing we have done so?" No, good instruction has always been the product of reflective practitioners articulating and meeting their objectives. Why settle for a hit-and-miss model of learning when Gardner and Noon give us such practical, empirical models to use? To integrate multiple intelligences theory and technology into instruction, one must aspire to become a technoconstructivist. Only at this level can teachers truly realize the full potential of every student in their charge.

Consider how Dana transformed her seventh-graders' study of the nervous system into a celebration of learning through different technologies. Figure 8 shows her preliminary flowchart. Table 26 shows the resulting unit plan.

FIGURE 8
Unit Plan Flowchart Example

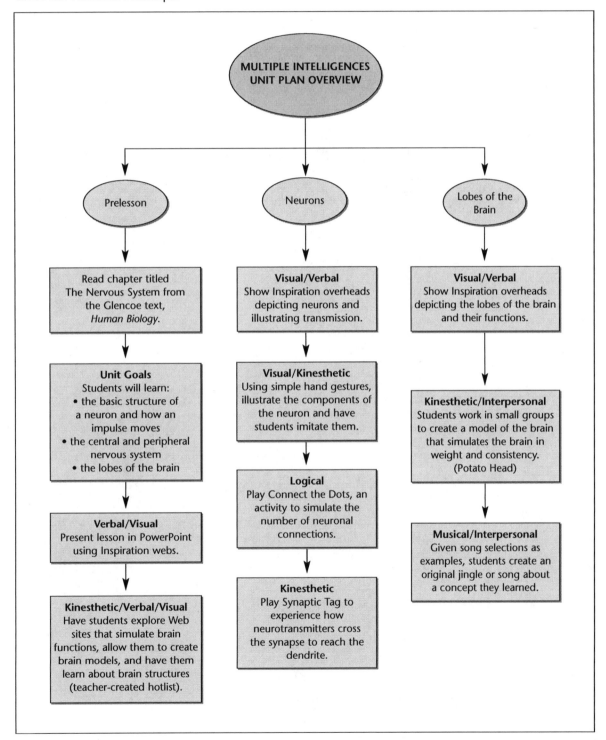

TABLE 26

Our Brain—The 3-Pound Wonder Unit

UNIT TITLE:	Our Brain—The 3-Pound Wonder
TEACHER:	Dana Topham, Ascension Day School, Lafayette, Louisiana
GRADE LEVEL:	7–8
SUBJECT(S):	Science **TIME FRAME:** 3 weeks

GOALS	INTELLIGENCES	TECHNOLOGIES	STANDARDS
• To learn the basic anatomy of the brain, including the cerebrum, cerebellum, and brain stem; the left and right hemispheres; and the lobes of the brain.	Verbal Logical Visual Kinesthetic Naturalist	PowerPoint Inspiration Browser	**NETS for Students:** **3. Technology productivity tools** • Students use productivity tools to collaborate in constructing technology-enhanced models, preparing publications, and producing other creative works.
• To explore the structure and function of neurons.	Logical Naturalist		

MATERIALS	INTELLIGENCES
Overhead	Visual
Computer	Kinesthetic
PowerPoint	Verbal Visual
Inspiration	Verbal Visual Naturalist
Web browser	Verbal Visual
Textbook: *Human Biology,* chapter titled The Nervous System (Glencoe, 1999)	Verbal Visual

PROCEDURE	
Preparation Have students read the Glencoe science chapter The Nervous System. Present a PowerPoint slideshow highlighting key facts of the brain's structure.	Visual Verbal
Have students explore hands-on Web sites through a teacher-created hotlist (www.kn.pacbell.com/wired/fil/pages/listthebraida.html).	Visual Verbal Kinesthetic

(Continued)

Our Brain—The 3-Pound Wonder Unit

(Continued)

PROCEDURE	INTELLIGENCES
Activities	
Present overheads depicting neurons and illustrating transmission for review of concepts.	Visual Verbal
Use simple hand gestures to illustrate the components of the neuron. Have students follow these instructions:	Kinesthetic

Use simple hand gestures to illustrate the components of the neuron. Have students follow these instructions:

> "Hold out your arm and spread your fingers. Your hand represents the 'cell body' (also called the 'soma'); your fingers represent 'dendrites' bringing information to the cell body; your arm represents the 'axon' taking information away from the cell body."
>
> (From *Neuroscience for Kids, Modeling the Nervous System, Simple Neuron Model*, http://faculty.washington.edu/chudler/chmodel.html)

Conduct "Connect the Dots," an activity to simulate the number of neuronal connections:

> "This exercise is to illustrate the complexity of the connections of the brain. Draw 10 dots on one side of a piece of paper and 10 dots on the other side of the paper. Assume these dots represent neurons, and assume that each neuron makes connections with the 10 dots on the other side of the paper. Then connect each dot on one side with the 10 dots on the other side. Remember that this is quite a simplification. Each neuron (dot) may actually make thousands of connections with other neurons. If you tried this your paper would be really messy!"
>
> (From *Neuroscience for Kids, Modeling the Nervous System, Connect the Dots*, http://faculty.washington.edu/chudler/chmodel.html)

(Intelligences: Logical)

Use the outside game "Synaptic Tag" to follow up on the concept of how neurotransmitters cross the synapse to reach the dendrite:

> "In the game of Synaptic Tag, you are part of the synapse. The object of the game is to get as many neurotransmitters across the synapse to the dendrite without being caught (deactivated) by the enzyme. It is like a game of tag. Draw or find a space for the axon and a dendrite (see the picture below). Some players are neurotransmitters and they wait in the axon; other players are enzymes and they wait in the gap between the axon and the dendrite. It is best to have more neurotransmitters than enzymes. The enzymes are 'it.' "

(Intelligences: Kinesthetic)

Axon — Neurotransmitters — Enzymes — Dendrite

> "When someone says 'go,' the neurotransmitters run across the synapse as fast as possible without being touched by an enzyme. If a neurotransmitter is touched by an enzyme, it must go back (be reabsorbed) into the axon and wait until the next turn. If a player makes it to the dendrite, the player is safe. Play as many times as you like. Make sure everyone has a chance to be a neurotransmitter and an enzyme."
>
> (From *Neuroscience for Kids, Outside Games, Synaptic Tag*, http://faculty.washington.edu/chudler/outside.html)

(Continued)

Our Brain—The 3-Pound Wonder Unit

(Continued)

PROCEDURE	INTELLIGENCES
Present overheads depicting lobes of the brain for review of concepts.	Visual Verbal
Have students work in small groups to create a model of the brain that simulates the brain in weight and consistency. Conduct the "Potato Head" activity: "This activity is meant to simulate the actual weight and size of a human brain. • 5 cups instant potato flakes • 2.5 cups hot water • 2 cups sand Combine all ingredients in a Ziploc bag and mix. It should weigh about 3 pounds and simulate the texture of a human brain." (From *Neuroscience for Kids, Modeling the Nervous System, Model a Brain*, http://faculty.washington.edu/chudler/chmodel.html)	Kinesthetic Interpersonal
Given song selections as examples, the students will create a new song or jingle about a concept they have learned. (From *Journey Into the Brain, Brainy Tunes*, www.morphonix.com/software/education/science/brain/game/songs/brainy_tunes.html)	Verbal Musical
Follow-Up Create a "brain" display and invite younger students to view the projects created. Pair students and allow them to "teach" the concepts to the younger students. The display should include student-created material, opportunities for exploring brain models, and other interactive materials.	

PRODUCT	
Working in pairs, the students will complete at least two projects: • Create a model of the brain using any selected medium (clay, Play-Doh, papier-mâché). The brain should be constructed according to scale and clearly depict the four lobes of the brain. Create a model of a neuron. It should include the axon, dendrites, and cell body.	Kinesthetic Logical Naturalist
• Make of recording of at least five brain songs (original or ones reviewed in class).	Musical
• Create three illustrations of the brain: (1) show the four lobes of the brain, (2) show the left and right hemispheres, (3) show the cerebrum, cerebellum, and brain stem.	Visual Naturalist
• Using simplified terminology, create a simple diagram of the lobes of the brain and their function, to be presented to a class of third-grade students. Be prepared to be the teacher and teach your minilesson	Visual Interpersonal Naturalist

ASSESSMENT	
Students will be evaluated on the two projects they complete: • Brain Model • Brain Songs • Brain Illustrations • Brain Lobes Diagram	Kinesthetic Logical Naturalist Musical Visual Interpersonal

Dana is clearly a blossoming technoconstructivist. Her varied classroom activities and use of technology to accomplish deeper student understanding speak well of her determination to make everyday learning a memorable event in her classroom.

How do we know when we have finally arrived as a technoconstructivist? It's a subjective judgment to some degree. I would argue that we never truly arrive; we simply keep working to evolve our instructional practices to more closely approximate the ideal. In short, I continue to aspire to be a technoconstructivist.

Traditional instructivist teaching takes less time than constructivist approaches. In this era of strict state standards and high-stakes testing, in which schools and teachers are held accountable for their students' performance on standardized tests, this seems like a tempting trade-off. Developing critical thinkers who take risks to solve problems in an environment where there isn't one right answer is a messy business. It's open-ended and time-consuming. Still, aren't all humans constructivist by nature? Don't we all discover meaning based on our own life experiences? Ultimately, each of us has to decide the business we are in: the business of test scores or the business of lifelong learning. What is your motivation as an educator? For me, it's seeing that spark light up in a struggling student's eyes, as it did for Jamie. Meaningful, engaging instruction creates motivated, lifelong learners—that is the true promise of technoconstructivism.

Resources for Further Study

Print

Carroll, J. A., Kelly, M. G., & Witherspoon, T. L. (2003). *NETS•S curriculum series: Multidisciplinary units for prekindergarten through grade 2.* Eugene, OR: International Society for Technology in Education.

Hannah, L. (Ed.). (2002). *NETS•S curriculum series: Multidisciplinary units for grades 3–5.* Eugene, OR: International Society for Technology in Education.

McKenzie, W., Archibald, D., Hutchison, M., Manweller, M., Moersch, C., Terry, P., & Jones Woods, C. (2004). *NETS•S curriculum series: Social studies units for grades 9–12.* Eugene, OR: International Society for Technology in Education.

O'Hara, S., & McMahon, M. (2003). *NETS•S curriculum series: Multidisciplinary units for grades 6–8.* Eugene, OR: International Society for Technology in Education.

Palloff, R. M., & Pratt, K. (2003). *The virtual student: A profile and guide to working with online learners.* Hoboken, NJ: Jossey-Bass.

Waterhouse, S. (2004). *The power of eLearning: The essential guide for teaching in the Digital Age.* Upper Saddle River, NJ: Allyn & Bacon.

Wenger, E., McDermott, R., & Snyder, W. M. (2002). *Cultivating communities of practice.* Cambridge, MA: Harvard Business School Press.

Online

Are You a Techno-Constructivist?:
www.educationworld.com/a_tech/tech/tech005.shtml

Constructivism: From Philosophy to Practice:
www.cdli.ca/~elmurphy/emurphy/cle.html

Creating a New Culture of Teaching and Learning:
www.anovember.com/articles/asilomar.html

Critical Friends Groups: Teachers Helping Teachers to Improve Student Learning:
www.pdkintl.org/edres/resbul28.htm

Drill the Teachers, Educate the Kids:
www.anovember.com/articles/drill.html

How Friends Can Be Critical as Schools Make Essential Changes:
http://ces.edgateway.net/cs/resources/view/ces_res/43

School Reform: What Role Can Technology Play in a Constructivist Setting?:
http://pixel.cs.vt.edu/edu/fis/techcons.html

Reflections

1 Where would you place yourself in Noon's model of teacher technology use?

2 How can a technotraditionalist accommodate the intelligences through technology? What limits or assists this?

3 Can you still keep your lessons compact and manageable as a technoconstructivist? Defend you answer.

4 What kind of support do you need to become a technoconstructivist?

CHAPTER 9

Internet-Based Instruction

Perhaps the most promising of all the digital technologies is the Internet. Whereas operating systems evolve in perpetuity and software is always being modified to offer something new and improved, the Internet operates free of any particular computer platform or private commercial interest. Within the connected classroom, the possible uses of the Internet are limited only by the teacher's vision and willingness to experiment.

Consider this Middle East WebQuest crafted by Sanaz Samali for her seventh graders (found online at **http://salem.k12.ma.us/schools/collins//technology/ Webquests%20and%20Links%20/Middle%20East.htm)**.

These are the instructions she gives to her class:

> *In this WebQuest, you will be exploring issues such as the roles of oil and water in the Middle East, religions of the Middle East, and the Israeli-Arab conflict. You are a team of journalists working for one of the world's most reputable and reliable news stations. You're on assignment in the heart of the Middle East. For the next few weeks you will be researching and exploring the different issues surrounding the Middle East. After your research is complete, you will give a live broadcast explaining the situation that you have researched, hoping to bring worldwide attention to these issues and raise the public's awareness about the Middle East.*

Ms. Samali's students will not only work in teams, conduct online research, and present newscasts that share their findings, they will also correspond with seventh graders in Iran by e-mail to help cultivate cross-cultural understanding. In an age when it is difficult to forge cross-cultural understanding among adults, Ms. Samali uses technology to create empathy and understanding among our next generation of citizens. The Internet provides us with powerful tools for doing this, and more.

By the Internet, I am referring to a variety of online technologies, as indicated in Table 27.

TABLE 27

Internet Technologies	
TECHNOLOGY	**INTELLIGENCES**
Electronic Mail (e-mail)	Verbal Interpersonal
Mailing Lists	Verbal Logical Interpersonal
Message Boards	Verbal Logical Interpersonal Naturalist
Chats	Verbal Visual Interpersonal Naturalist Existential

(Continued)

TECHNOLOGY	INTELLIGENCES
Internet Technologies *(Continued)*	
Multiuser Virtual Environments (MUVEs)	Verbal Logical Visual Kinesthetic Interpersonal Intrapersonal Naturalist Existential
World Wide Web (WWW)	Verbal Logical Visual Musical Kinesthetic Interpersonal Intrapersonal Naturalist Existential

The Internet is more than just Web sites. It is an interconnected virtual community made up of all kinds of multimedia information, interaction, and collaboration. By its very nature, the Internet is the most robust medium for addressing all the intelligences. It supports them seamlessly, in concert with each individual's ability level. Because of its sophisticated structure, let's take a closer look at its components before discussing its instructional implications.

There are two kinds of collaboration online, asynchronous (independent of time constraints) and synchronous (time dependent or conducted in real time).

Asynchronous Communication

Asynchronous forms of online communication include electronic mail, mailing lists, and message boards. Asynchronous communication affords the user the luxury of posting and responding to messages at any time, from any location that has an Internet connection. It is popular because it allows users to interact free of time constraints. You don't have to be online at 7:00 p.m. on a Thursday night in order to meet with your peers. New messages will be there for you to find whenever you have the time to view them. You can check your e-mail or log in to a newsgroup at any hour on any day of the week and catch up on the most recent messages posted by colleagues. Asynchronous communication can be used in instruction in various ways.

Electronic Mail

Many classes have used e-mail to correspond with students from other parts of the world as "keypals" (keyboard penpals). Teachers correspond with one another to plan writing tasks between the classes. The evolving relationship can include picture files shared as e-mail attachments, digital video greetings, and packages of materials sent by "snail" mail. When classes are within close proximity, end-of-year trips to visit one another are also a popular practice. A number of services online can help you screen prospective classes for keypals, including ePals (**www.epals.com**), Gaggle (**www.gaggle.net**), and the Keypals Club (**www.teaching.com/keypals/**).

E-mail projects are also popular among connected classrooms. Remember the Great Mail Race Project of the early 1990s in which classes snail-mailed letters to "Any School" c/o a random ZIP code in every state? They waited to hear back from all 50 states and charted the responses they received in the classroom. Classes conduct a modified version of this project in today's classroom, sending electronic mailings to schools around the country or even around the world. The resulting interaction between classes promotes language arts, social studies, mathematics, science, and even health. Cooperating teachers can plan topics for students to write on, projects in which they share data, exchanges of information about communities and countries, and much, much more.

The Flat Stanley Project (**www.enoreo.on.ca/flatstanley/index.htm**) is another example of a snail-mail phenomenon that has taken on a new life online. Based on a character in a book by Jeff Brown, Flat Stanley is a boy who is flattened by a billboard so completely that he is able to travel by being folded and mailed. Students contact fellow Internet travelers from around the world to send them a replica of Flat Stanley. Recipients of a Flat Stanley take him along on their daily tasks and keep a record of their adventures together. They then send an account of Stanley's visit back to the class from which Stanley came. Now, however, it can all be done online using e-mail and a digital camera. Think of the money a class can save just on postage!

Ask-an-expert services are another great way to use e-mail. Consider studying the solar system and having your students e-mail a NASA scientist when they have a question they can't find an answer to in the resources available at school, or e-mailing a USGS geologist when they want to learn more about plate tectonics. Ask-an-expert services allow you to do just that. They are typically free of charge, and often require a week or two before you get a response. But the result is worth the wait when your classroom comes alive with the response from an actual expert in your class's studies. To find out more about these services, simply go to your favorite search engine and conduct a search on "ask an expert." You'll be amazed at the results!

E-mail projects tend to promote the verbal and interpersonal intelligences most prominently. They rely on a commitment to stay in touch and respond on a regular basis, so teachers and students who are "people people" and find writing a pleasant, easy task will enjoy participating in them. E-mail projects are also an excellent way to promote the verbal and interpersonal intelligences in students who may need to more fully develop these paths to learning. The one caveat for teachers is that e-mail projects require a lot of monitoring. You will want to conference with your students and know their status in the project. Furthermore, if you have a strict acceptable use policy (AUP), you will need to screen correspondence. Be sure you know your school's AUP!

Mailing Lists

Mailing lists can be very useful in conducting classroom projects. While it is not necessarily a project unto itself, a well-constructed mailing list can augment a project by creating a virtual community online. For example, if you are collaborating with other classes online, adding all the students' e-mail addresses to a mailing list allows anyone on the list to send out one e-mail that is automatically delivered to everyone on the list. This can be very handy when making an announcement, posing a general question, or sharing information.

A mailing list is set up with one common e-mail address to which everyone can send announcements. When an e-mail is sent to that address, it is then distributed to everyone. It is best to have a moderator for a project mailing list, someone who screens all mailings sent to the list's common address before they are posted. This helps keep the list free of off-topic discussions and misinformation. The moderator also can add members to and delete them from the mailing list, keeping it a safe, private community. Most important, mailing lists are password protected, so you can maintain a closed community without stray visitors having access to your archives.

Mailing lists tend to stimulate the verbal, interpersonal, and existential intelligences. Their communal nature really helps students feel part of something bigger, and the lists are still largely a haven for those who like to write and interact. Nonetheless, mailing lists also have a business-like function as members keep one another informed and up to date on project happenings.

Consider the technology coordinators' mailing list moderated by Tim Landeck of Santa Cruz, California. This list is an asynchronous forum for instructional technology coordinators to pose questions, generate possible solutions, and share experiences common to the group. When a member posts a question, it is sent out to everyone on the list. Colleagues can then respond by e-mail with their recommendations, which are also distributed to everyone on the list. If the problem is cut and dried, such as setting up a school mail server, the list may see a small flourish of activity on the topic and then quiet down again. However, when a more controversial topic comes up, such as using filtering software, the activity level on the list may increase sharply as e-mails are posted to the list in response to different points of view.

Regardless of the topic, a sense of belonging and commitment to the group develops over time. Members of the list belong to a community that they can access any time or day (existential). They can brainstorm ideas (visual) and solve problems (logical) while getting to know one another as online friends (interpersonal). Moreover, because it is a list specifically for technology coordinators, there is a common set of values and concerns shared on the list (intrapersonal). It is truly a cyber support group.

Message Boards

Message boards can include discussion groups, newsgroups, and even archived mailing lists. While an e-mail comes to you, a message board is housed at a fixed Internet address that you must visit in order to participate. Some message board services will notify you by e-mail when new messages have been posted, but you still have to log in to the virtual location to read and respond.

The dynamic of a message board is that interaction takes place among a finite set of participants, so a virtual community is built over time. Not everyone has to agree or get along, but over time they all get to know one another well through their exchanges. Each message board community tends to cultivate its own culture as it evolves, which may include a recorded history, an inside humor, and expressions and shorthand unique to that group.

Moreover, message boards are archived at their virtual location. You can go back and look through a certain topic or "thread" that was discussed and read all the messages from its initial posting to its conclusion. The metaphor of a thread serves message boards well, as each individual thread on a board is woven into the fabric that becomes the community identified with it. Because of this archive feature, message boards not only serve the verbal, interpersonal, and existential intelligences, they also accommodate the naturalist intelligence well. Message board archives provide a structure and organization that allow the naturalist learner in all of us to make sense of digital, text-based communication.

The Teacher to Teacher (T2T) community has switched from mailing lists to message boards for just these reasons. Now when you subscribe to this service, instead of getting several daily mailings (verbal) you can simply log in to the site and participate on the boards that address your professional interests (intrapersonal). Threads develop and evolve as the group sees the need to pursue pertinent topics (interpersonal), and the sense of community at T2T is very tangible—even to a first-time visitor (existential). Because the message board is asynchronous, you can log in any time of the day or go for weeks without checking in and then catch up all at once (musical). The true mark of a message board community is that once you participate on a board that is of particular interest to you, it is very difficult to stop participating or to remove yourself completely from the board. The feeling of belonging keeps you coming back!

Synchronous Communication

Synchronous communication includes real-time chat and multiuser virtual environments (MUVEs). The hallmark of synchronous communication is that it takes place in "real time." In other words, when you post a message, it is read at the exact moment it is posted. You then read responses from others within seconds of posting your idea. It is the text-based version of face-to-face conversation: spontaneous, fast paced, and dynamic. While asynchronous forms of communication seem passive by nature, synchronous interaction is active and engaging. It requires that the parties involved be online at the same moment regardless of location or time zone to communicate with each other using text.

Chat

There are a number of ways to chat online, including Web site-based chat, Internet relay chat (IRC), and instant messaging chat. Web site-based chat is extremely common nowadays, as Java applets have made it very easy to offer chat on a Web page. This phenomenon has become commonplace enough that these chat rooms are free, usually only requiring you to register for security purposes. Web site-based chat is typically social in nature, and participants come and go without necessarily feeling a sense of belonging. Usually a core group of familiar users faithfully return to a specific site, but they are outnumbered by the visitors who come to see what the chat is all about and then move on. Even the more sophisticated Web site-based chats that propose themes of common interest tend to have a low rate of success in building a large core of repeat users. Community is hard to build this way.

Internet relay chat requires the installation of software to help you connect to the Internet and make use of a custom-designed chat interface. The software is usually free and so is the chat. Once you have set up the software on your system, you simply log in and set up your personal profile. You can then access thousands of chats by topic, bookmark those chat rooms you wish to revisit, and even create your own room if you desire. Unlike Web site-based chats, IRC tends to build strong core groups of participants that resemble minicommunities. These core groups, however, are not necessarily tied to just one chat room: instead, they frequently move among rooms while still remaining an identifiable group. The culture created through IRC has very few boundaries, so you will come across every kind of topic imaginable. This often makes it an inappropriate environment for children.

More familiar to the general public are the chat services provided by national Internet service providers (ISPs) such as CompuServe, the Microsoft Network, and America Online. (Did you know that America Online started out as a message board?) These services also require you to install software, but there is a monthly subscriber fee and terms of service that set boundaries on the topics and behavior that are allowed in the chat areas. Like IRC, a variety of chat rooms are available and users can create their own if they wish, but the rooms do not number in the thousands and the topics conform to the more generally held mores and conventions of society. Again, you may find core members referred to as "regulars" in these ISP chats, but the bulk of a chat room's traffic consists of transient visitors just looking to see what is happening.

Recently, a variety of instant messaging applications have become available that are quickly becoming the most popular way to chat. They are usually free and include such names as ICQ, Instant Messenger, and Yahoo Messenger. These tools connect to the Internet whenever you do and let you know when friends are online. You can send messages back and forth privately without having to log in to a chat room, and you can even record and save your messages. Moreover, you can conduct an instant message chat while working in other applications because the chat interface is a small window that does not block your view of other programs you may have running. There's a nice sense of control with instant messaging because you offer your username only to those people you want to be able to contact you, and you can block access of users with whom you do not wish to chat. There is a very low incidence of transient traffic interrupting these private chats. Also, you can chat as a group using instant messaging, so the notion of having to be tied down to a virtual chat room is becoming obsolete.

Like asynchronous communication, synchronous chat is a text-based function that is limited in what it can offer the user. You can interact in real time. In some cases you can exchange files. But the potential for more than the interaction of ideas in a social forum is limited. Synchronous interaction often has the effect of lowering people's inhibitions, allowing them to act out in ways they would never behave face to face. In fact, because of the benefits chat offers, it has carved an online niche for itself in which it is seen as a tool for fun and exploration. More sophisticated MUVE participants are easily insulted when MUVEs are referred to as "chat rooms," but if you log in to any chat community you will note the high level of activity and the volume of people using the service. Chat is the offbeat cousin no one likes to mention in the family of synchronous communication services.

The verbal, interpersonal, and existential intelligences are easily stimulated by synchronous chat. To make broader use of a chat environment, you would need to have a task-oriented group of people using the interface for a specific goal. For example, if you have a group of teachers from geographically remote locations meet on IRC to critique and recommend software applications for a conference presentation they are planning, they would quickly use their logical and intrapersonal intelligences as well. It always comes back to the context in which the application is used. The context dictates which intelligences are in play.

MUVEs

If chats are the lowbrow version of synchronous communication, MUVEs are the highbrow. In a MUVE you can communicate in text in real time, move through virtual spaces, create your own virtual persona, and work collaboratively to complete tasks. A large part of a MUVE is the metaphor used to create this virtual world. A MUVE can use the metaphor of a college campus, a castle, an amusement park, or any other environment familiar to us in the real world. In entering a MUVE, you immerse yourself in its metaphor and learn to function accordingly. You create a persona that will be accepted there. For example, in a castle metaphor you would want to create a persona consistent with a castle's theme: a knight, prince, lady, or duchess. You can create or select an image that represents you in the MUVE so that people will recognize you, and that persona will help define your place in this virtual world.

A good example of a MUVE is TappedIn, or TI (**http://ti2.sri.com/tappedin/**), which is designed as a virtual world for educators. Its metaphor is an office tower with adjacent buildings, in which you can have your own office space and participate in public discussions and activities. When you first enter TI, you are welcomed at the help desk. You can make your way quickly to an office or the auditorium if you are there for a scheduled event, or you can leisurely meet colleagues as you move from room to room. You can "see" only colleagues who are in the same "room" that you are in, although you can find others through various functions that TI offers.

Because it is designed for professional educators, TI has a number of features that promote interaction and collaboration. Participants can store and save files, use a "tape recorder" that will record discussions and archive them for future reference, create "notes" they can call up on command to explain ideas to others, and even project Web sites that everyone in the room can see and discuss together. As a MUVE, TI addresses a number of intelligences:

Verbal. Text-based communication

Logical. File storage, scheduled events, structured environment

Visual. Navigating through virtual rooms, sharing Web sites

Interpersonal. Collaboration with colleagues

Naturalist. Community hierarchy and classification of archived files

Existential. Belonging to a virtual community

TI also has a Student Activity Center that allows teachers to bring in their classes to work online in a safe, controlled environment. Teachers create student IDs under their own TI username, and students don't have access to any other part of TI except the Student Activity Center.

Several years ago my fourth graders were the first class to use the TI Student Activity Center. We were collaborating with seventh graders at a middle school 90 minutes north of us in Virginia to research Thomas Jefferson and create a Web site presenting his accomplishments.

Because of the physical distance between the two schools, we could not collaborate face to face. Because of the visual nature of the project, e-mail and chat were only of limited use. TappedIn offered a solution to our needs.

We were able to meet in the Student Activity Center in six small groups because the center houses six small studios. I created six tape recorders and placed one in each studio so that each work session would be recorded while my counterpart and I moved from studio to studio, spot-checking group work and helping out when needed. At the end of the session, all tape-recorded transcripts were automatically e-mailed directly to me so that they could be distributed to the groups as they continued working separately.

The project came together well. We knew it was a success once students began putting together whole pages on Jefferson's childhood, education, inventions, accomplishments, and presidency. You can see the final product at **http://surfaquarium.com/PP/Jefferson/**. We capped off the project and the school year by meeting at Camden Yards in June to watch an Orioles game and finally put names and faces together after all our online work! MUVEs are a wonderful way to promote a variety of intelligences online.

Collaborative Online Projects

Because of its multimedia, interactive nature, the Web is an excellent environment for collaboration among students of disparate geographical locations. While teachers may set up online research projects that remain within the four walls of their classroom, the true potential of this new medium is tapped when teachers engage their class with students from other locations around the nation, and even around the world. Collaborative online projects offer the possibility of developing students' higher order thinking skills and accommodating all the intelligences by combining on- and offline resources. They can take many forms, as evidenced by my list of projects at the Surfaquarium (**http://surfaquarium.com/Projects/**). Collaborative online projects are multidisciplinary and multi-intelligence. They can be:

- classroom centered
- Web based
- challenges
- contests
- task oriented
- data driven
- time sensitive
- ongoing
- asynchronous
- synchronous

Collaborative online projects are typically designed by teachers who are looking for like-minded colleagues to join their classes and complete a project together. Once a teacher has designed a project, he or she announces it through teacher mailing lists and project archives such as Global Schoolhouse (**www.gsn.org/GSH/pr/_cfm/index.cfm**). This helps recruit other classes for the project. The following elements should be considered when designing an online project:

Goals. State the purpose of the project up front so interested teachers will know what the project entails.

Timeline. Outline specific dates for registration and each subsequent stage of the project so teachers will know how it is paced.

Resources. Name specific resources the teacher will need to have access to in order to participate: Internet connection, hardware, software, hands-on materials, texts, and so on.

Final Product. Describe the final product participating classes will create for the project.

Project Web Site. Create a Web site that participating classes can visit at any time to go over project information and announcements and share ideas and final products.

Contact Person. Provide an e-mail address where the sponsoring teacher can be reached.

To maximize your collaborative online project for MI, you will want to follow these steps:

1 Create the outline for the project.

2 Identify the intelligences stimulated by the project tasks you have outlined.

3 Edit and revise your outline to accommodate all the intended intelligences.

A Collaborative Online Project Template

Table 28 presents a template for creating a collaborative online project.

TABLE 28

Multiple Intelligences Collaborative Online Project Template

COLLABORATIVE ONLINE PROJECT TITLE:

TEACHER:

GRADE LEVEL:

SUBJECT(S):   TIME FRAME:

GOALS	INTELLIGENCES	TECHNOLOGIES	STANDARDS
			(NETS, subject, and state standards)

TIMELINE

MATERIALS	INTELLIGENCES
PROCEDURE	
PRODUCT	
ASSESSMENT	

Consider the eIditarod project I sponsor (**http://surfaquarium.com/eIDITAROD/**) at the Surfaquarium. Classes are invited to follow the Iditarod Sled Dog Race in March by studying the race using online resources, following a musher of their choosing, and writing to the musher on- and offline. It brings together the study of animals, weather, geography, mapping, elapsed time, letter writing, e-mail, and problem solving in one high-interest collection of activities. The full project entails much more than that, though, as evidenced by the plan outlined in Table 29.

TABLE 29

The eIditarod Collaborative Online Project

COLLABORATIVE ONLINE PROJECT TITLE: The eIditarod
TEACHER: McKenzie
GRADE LEVEL: 7–8
SUBJECT(S):   Language Arts, Math, Science, Social Studies   **TIME FRAME:** 3 months

GOALS	INTELLIGENCES	TECHNOLOGIES	STANDARDS
• Students will follow a musher through the Iditarod Sled Dog Race using the World Wide Web, and write to the musher at the conclusion of the race.	Verbal Logical Visual Musical Kinesthetic Interpersonal Intrapersonal Naturalist Existential	Internet Browser Microsoft Office	**NETS for Students:** **2. Social, ethical, and human issues** • Students develop positive attitudes toward technology uses that support lifelong learning, collaboration, personal pursuits, and productivity. **3. Technology productivity tools** • Students use technology tools to enhance learning, increase productivity, and promote creativity. **4. Technology communications tools** • Students use a variety of media and formats to communicate information and ideas effectively to multiple audiences.

(Continued)

The elditarod Collaborative Online Project

(Continued)

GOALS	INTELLIGENCES	TECHNOLOGIES	STANDARDS
			5. Technology research tools • Students use technology to locate, evaluate, and collect information from a variety of sources. • Students evaluate and select new information resources and technological innovations based on the appropriateness to specific tasks. **6. Technology problem-solving and decision-making tools** • Students use technology resources for solving problems and making informed decisions. • Students use technology to make appropriate choices based on the data provided.

TIMELINE

January 8–26	Open registration period for classes to join the project.
January 29–February 9	Students create a wall map of the trail.
February 11–February 23	Students select a musher to follow in the race.
February 26–March 2	Students study and prepare your class for the big event.
March 3–end of the race	Students follow their musher and send an e-mail at each checkpoint.
March 31	Students post their final written task to the project Web site.

MATERIALS

The Official Iditarod Trail Committee Web Site: www.iditarod.com

The Official elditarod Mailing List: http://groups.yahoo.com/group/eiditarod

The Official elditarod Project Web Site: http://surfaquarium.com/elDITAROD/

INTELLIGENCES

Verbal
Logical
Visual
Musical
Naturalist
Intrapersonal
Interpersonal
Naturalist
Existential

(Continued)

The elditarod Collaborative Online Project

(Continued)

PROCEDURE	INTELLIGENCES
1 Students study the trail's geography and read musher biographies.	Verbal Logical Naturalist
2 Students create a wall-sized map of the trail using a grid and a compass rose.	Visual Logical Kinesthetic Naturalist
3 Students select a musher to follow in the race.	Intrapersonal
4 Students track on the wall map the selected musher's progress and weather conditions during the race.	Logical Musical Existential
5 Students send an e-mail to each checkpoint that the selected musher reaches on the trail.	Verbal Interpersonal
6 Students receive a response from the organizers at the project Web site each time they write.	Verbal Interpersonal
7 With support from the classroom teacher, students complete the problem-solving tasks sent from the project Web site by e-mail.	Logical Interpersonal Musical Naturalist
8 Students arrive in Nome vicariously with their selected musher.	Logical Existential
9 Students submit a letter to their musher for publication on the project Web site.	Verbal Intrapersonal Existential
PRODUCT	
Students send a letter to the musher they selected, sharing their new knowledge and experiences in following the race.	Verbal Interpersonal Intrapersonal Existential
ASSESSMENT	
Teachers can assess student learning based on the criteria that flows naturally from the prescribed curriculum they follow.	Verbal Interpersonal Intrapersonal Existential

Note how the project stimulates all nine intelligences. Problem-solving tasks e-mailed to classes during the race include determining ways to get additional snow on the trail where it had melted as a result of unusually warm temperatures, making plans for spacing out required rest stops on the trail so a dog team had the best chance to win, offering suggestions for the number of dogs to use during different phases of the race to maximize sled speed, designing and building dog sleds using craft sticks, making Inuit carvings out of soap, and building igloos out of sugar cubes.

The project has grown from approximately 125 classes its first year to more than 500 classes from around the world in 2004. Visit the project Web site to see examples of student work and the final letters to mushers. Because it involves a high-interest topic and all the intelligences, it has been a successful project for everyone involved. Have your own idea for a great collaborative online project? Plug it into the template and you'll be well on your way to success.

There is no more effective way to empower teachers to use the Internet than by giving them the tools to be successful. Marge Shasberger did just that by creating a unit that introduced the wealth of the Internet to her colleagues (Table 30). It involves all the intelligences and employs a variety of technologies.

TABLE 30

Teachers on the Web Collaborative Online Project

COLLABORATIVE ONLINE PROJECT TITLE: Teachers on the Web
TEACHER: Marge Shasberger, Placer County Office of Education, Auburn, California
GRADE LEVEL: Adult Education
SUBJECT(S): Staff Development   **TIME FRAME:** 5 days (1 week)

GOALS	INTELLIGENCES	TECHNOLOGIES	STANDARDS
Teachers will be able to use the Internet as a viable resource in the classroom. Teachers will show proficiency by: • Demonstrating the ability to use search tools, to access major Internet resource sites, and to properly use and cite cyber information.	Verbal Logical Visual Naturalist Existential	Browser	**Proposed California Performance Standards for Educators— Technology** (http://ctap.k12.ca.us/ grants/teachstds.html) **Level One— Personal Proficiency A** Performance Standards 1, 2, 3, 5, 6

(Continued)

Teachers on the Web Collaborative Online Project

(Continued)

GOALS	INTELLIGENCES	TECHNOLOGIES	STANDARDS
• Showing the ability to use e-mail, listservs, and bulletin boards for communication in the classroom with students or experts in a field, and for their own professional growth through communication with other teachers as a support/informational group.	Verbal Logical Visual Interpersonal Intrapersonal Naturalist Existential	Browser Mail client	**Level Two—** **Instructional Proficiency** **A** Performance Standards 1, 2, 3, 5 **B** Initial Assessment A-4
• Explaining the possibilities available to students for various forms of presentations and the expression of ideas and concepts learned in a lesson.	Verbal Logical Visual Musical Kinesthetic Interpersonal Intrapersonal Naturalist Existential	Presentation software, multimedia software, text and graphics software	**Level Three—** **Mentor Proficiency** **A** Performance Standards 1, 2, 3, 4, 5 **Level Four—** **Leadership Proficiency** **A** Performance Expectations 1, 2

TIMELINE

Day 1	Introduction to the Internet and the World Wide Web
Day 2	Introduction to Presentation Software
Day 3	Preliminary Group Work
Day 4	Ongoing Group Work
Day 5	Class Presentations

MATERIALS	INTELLIGENCES
Hardware Computers	Kinesthetic
Printers	Visual
Projection equipment	Visual
Digital cameras	Visual
Camcorders	Visual Verbal

(Continued)

Teachers on the Web Collaborative Online Project

(Continued)

MATERIALS	INTELLIGENCES
Software Browser	Verbal Visual Interpersonal Existential
Mail client	Verbal Visual Interpersonal Existential
Presentation software	Verbal Visual Musical Kinesthetic
Multimedia software	Verbal Visual Musical Kinesthetic
Text and graphics software	Verbal Visual
Other Materials Hotlists for resource sites	Verbal Logical Naturalist Existential
Art supplies	Visual Kinesthetic

PROCEDURE

Preparation
Preparation will include developing sample scavenger hunts, hotlists, rules for using the Internet (searching techniques, using e-mail, downloading materials, citing sources, and so forth), sample rubrics for evaluating Web sites and classroom projects, sample lesson outlines, and sample lessons.

Activities
Day 1: Introduction to the Internet and the World Wide Web

Hour 1: Greetings and introductions. Overview of class activities and expectations. Class will take the MI survey.	Logical Intrapersonal
Hours 2–4: Introduction to the Internet and the World Wide Web.	
Brief history and explanation of the Internet and the World Wide Web.	Verbal
Discussion of basic terms and tools for using the World Wide Web, including the use of and similarities and differences among search engines, directories, and other tools.	Verbal Interpersonal
• Activity 1: Students will practice ways to search effectively, using prepared subject sheets and visiting search sites.	Verbal Logical

(Continued)

Teachers on the Web Collaborative Online Project

(Continued)

PROCEDURE	INTELLIGENCES
• Activity 2: Students will visit various informational sites that give instructions on searching, such as Kathy Schrock's site (www.capecod.net/schrockguide/yp/iypsrch.htm), the Computer Strategies site (www.compstrategies.com/resources/search.html), and the Eureka site (www.gocee.com/eureka/eureka_i.htm).	Verbal Logical
Demonstration of basic classroom applications including scavenger hunts, research hotlists, independent searches for information, and proper preparation of activities for classroom use. The class will discuss ethical and legal issues involved in using the Internet and WWW as a resource and informational tool.	Verbal Intrapersonal
• Activity 3: Students will complete a sample scavenger hunt prepared by the teacher, then choose a subject of interest and prepare a scavenger hunt of their own as a result of their search experiences. Students will explore various teacher resource sites, including Education World (www.education-world.com), Computer Strategies (www.compstrategies.com/resources/k12edsites.html), Dewpoint (http://ivory.lm.com/~mundie/DDHC/DDH.htm), Global School Network (www.gsn.org/wce), and the George Lucas Foundation (www.glef.org).	Logical Visual
Hours 5–6: Using e-mail, listservs, and other communication sources such as bulletin boards, the class will review the various methods of participating in dialogues with other users.	Verbal Existential
• Activity 1: The class will e-mail messages to each other.	Verbal Interpersonal
• Activity 2: The class will explore the listservs available on Lizst, the mailing list directory (www.liszt.com), and Education World (www.education-world.com). Students will subscribe to at least one location of their choice.	Logical Intrapersonal
• Activity 3: The class will explore the Scholastic Web site, locating an active bulletin board of their choice for discussion.	Verbal Intrapersonal
• Activity 4: The class will explore e-mail and project Web sites for classroom participation, such as Classroom Connect (www.classroom.com/home.asp).	Logical Intrapersonal Existential
Day 2: Introduction to Presentation Software	
Hours 1–3: The class will review the basic tools and procedures used to effectively prepare a PowerPoint presentation.	
• Activity 1: Using prepared slide presentations, students will practice modifying a slideshow by changing text, adding a slide, and importing graphics. They will become familiar with PowerPoint template slides, design templates, and presentation templates.	Logical Kinesthetic
• Activity 2: Using the Outline View, students will prepare an outline of their lives. This will include such main topics as the individual's history, personal information (likes, dislikes, place of residence, family makeup), educational background, teaching experience, and goals for this class.	Verbal Logical Visual Musical Kinesthetic

(Continued)

Teachers on the Web Collaborative Online Project

(Continued)

PROCEDURE	INTELLIGENCES
Hours 4–6: The class will explore advanced techniques including creating slide transitions, animation, and backgrounds, and importing outside resources (such as graphics and text from Word, the Internet, and digital cameras).	
• Activity 1: The class will explore slide effects using a prepared slideshow.	Visual
• Activity 2: The class will apply slide effects to individual information outlines.	Visual
• Activity 3: The class will present their slideshows.	Verbal Visual Musical
Day 3: Preliminary Group Work The class will be divided as evenly as possible into groups made up of different intelligences. Assignments will include preparing a lesson in a subject area of the group's choice for use in a classroom.	
Hours 1–3: Groups will be formed. Each group will choose the subject or theme for the lesson to be presented to the class. The group will establish an objective for the lesson, decide on the method of presenting the lesson to the class, and determine the types of resources to be used (searches, project sites, e-mail, and so forth).	Verbal Logical Interpersonal Intrapersonal
Hours 4–6: At the beginning of the afternoon session, each group will be asked to outline the basic idea it has decided to work on, including the assignment for each group member. Each group will indicate how it intends to use the technology as a tool in the lesson it is preparing. The remainder of the afternoon will be spent preparing the group activity.	Verbal Naturalist
Day 4: Ongoing Group Work *Hours 1–3:* Groups will continue activities related to their projects.	Verbal Interpersonal
Hours 4–6: Using the class as a sample student population, groups will complete their class presentations and activities to demonstrate how technology will be used in their lessons.	Intrapersonal Interpersonal
Day 5: Class Presentations Groups will present their individual class projects, including activities in which students would be required to participate if the lesson were offered in a school environment.	Verbal Visual Musical
Groups will assess their peer presenters, offering feedback and suggestions.	Intrapersonal Interpersonal

(Continued)

Teachers on the Web Collaborative Online Project

(Continued)

PRODUCT	INTELLIGENCES
Groups will develop and present projects that demonstrate the use of technology in lessons.	Verbal Logical Visual Musical Kinesthetic Interpersonal Intrapersonal Naturalist Existential

ASSESSMENT

A rubric based on the following criteria will be used to evaluate the participants.

Technology Tools

1 The group did not demonstrate a basic understanding of the use of technology tools (search engines, e-mail, multimedia software) to maximize Internet use in the classroom.

2 The group demonstrated a basic understanding of the use of technology tools (search engines, e-mail, multimedia software) and the application of these tools to effectively navigate and use the Internet in the classroom.

3 The group exhibited a clear understanding of the use of technology tools (search engines, e-mail, multimedia software) and the application of these tools to effectively navigate and use the Internet in the classroom.

[Intelligences: Interpersonal, Logical, Existential]

Integration

1 The group project did not demonstrate a basic understanding of the Internet as a useful resource tool.

2 The group project demonstrated a basic understanding of the Internet as a useful research tool.

3 The group project demonstrated a superior understanding of the Internet as a useful research tool.

[Intelligences: Verbal, Interpersonal, Logical, Existential]

Presentation

1 The final presentation did not discuss technology in its content, nor did it depend on technology for its delivery to the class.

2 The final presentation utilized a minimum of one technology resource.

3 The final presentation utilized several technology resources to enhance the lesson and maximize interaction by the students.

[Intelligences: Verbal, Visual, Interpersonal, Logical, Musical, Existential]

Lesson

1 The final project allowed for the optional use of technology for the lesson. The class was not actively involved.

2 The final project encouraged the use of technology as a resource for the lesson, and included a basic outline of activities to further this use. Class participation was encouraged.

[Intelligences: Logical, Interpersonal, Naturalist, Existential]

(Continued)

Teachers on the Web Collaborative Online Project

(Continued)

ASSESSMENT	INTELLIGENCES
3 The final project included firm goals requiring the use of technology as an essential tool in the research, implementation, and presentation of the lesson. Class participation was ongoing and interactive. The class experimented with all aspects of the proposed lesson.	
Multiple Intelligences **1** The group activity demonstrated a single vision or presentation style.	Verbal Logical Visual
2 The group activity showed the input of several different learning and teaching methods.	Kinesthetic Musical
3 The group activity was presented to the class in several different ways, such as a well-thought-out research hotlist, an exciting slideshow presentation, and an artistic class handout, allowing the class to participate in different activities and demonstrating the input and skill of the various group members.	Interpersonal Intrapersonal Naturalist Existential

Ms. Shasberger has created a powerful set of learning experiences for teachers that involve a combination of intelligences and technologies. By using these different Internet-based technologies, they will be ready to work and learn online with their students. Note that Ms. Shasberger includes consideration of the intelligences used in her assessment rubric for student final projects. Multiple intelligences can be a body of knowledge for students to master as well as a process they see within themselves!

Resources for Further Study

Print

Barab, S., Kling, R., Gray, J. H., Pea, R., Brown, J. S., & Heath, C. (Eds.). (2004). *Designing for virtual communities in the service of learning (Learning in doing: Social, cognitive and computational perspectives)*. Cambridge: Cambridge University Press.

Cole, C., Ray, K., & Zanetis, J. (2004). *Videoconferencing for K–12 classrooms: A program development guide*. Eugene, OR: International Society for Technology in Education.

Gramling, A., Curtis, M., Reese, K., Wieczorek, A., Norris, C., & Soloway, E. (2004). *Pocket PC computers: A complete resource for classroom teachers*. Eugene, OR: International Society for Technology in Education.

Parker Roerden, L. (2003). *Net lessons: Web-based projects for your classroom*. Sebastopol, CA: O'Reilly & Associates.

Shank, P., & Sitze, A. (2004). *Making sense of online learning: A guide for beginners and the truly skeptical*. Hoboken, NJ: John Wiley & Sons.

Sharp, V. F., Levine, M. G., & Sharp, R. M. (2002). *The best Web sites for teachers* (5th ed.). Eugene, OR: International Society for Technology in Education.

Wenger, E. (1999). *Communities of practice: Learning, meaning, and identity.* Cambridge: Cambridge University Press.

Online

Hand-Held Devices in the Classroom:
http://eduscapes.com/tap/topic78.htm

The Internet as Curriculum:
www.fno.org/jan97/curriculum.html

Online Projects:
http://surfaquarium.com/IT/project.htm

Scavenger Hunts:
www.pitt.edu/~poole/eledScavenger.html

Virtual Field Trips:
www.uen.org/utahlink/tours/

The Web: Teaching Zack to Think:
www.anovember.com/articles/zack.html

WebQuests:
http://webquest.sdsu.edu

Reflections

1   Which forms of synchronous and asynchronous communication would work well with your learners and curriculum?

2   Identify the eIditarod project's level of technology integration on Noon's scale and explain your reasoning.

3   Which topics in your curriculum could you develop into a Web-based project?

4   Which is more desirable: a Web-based project designed for a one-computer classroom or a similar project designed for a computer lab? Defend your answer.

CHAPTER **10**

Assessment

The hallmark of a great lesson, unit, or project is its results. Say what you will about the latest and greatest technology or the newest trend to come down the pike; master teachers know that it all is for naught if instruction doesn't lead to mastery of a learning objective. In fact, veteran teachers can be the hardest group to sell a new idea to, not because they are unwilling to expand on their repertoire of strategies but because they've seen so many bandwagons pass by their classroom, never to be heard from again. If it is worthwhile and it works, it will find its way through their door. The proof is in the performance, and assessments measure performance.

hat has been so remarkable about Howard Gardner's work from the beginning is that Gardner did not try to package MI theory to mass-produce teaching kits for profit, nor did he promise educators it would revolutionize the way they look at teaching and learning. Instead, educators approached Gardner, asking how his theory could be applied and what it could mean for schools. In his disarming, unassuming way, Gardner has responded that he leaves it up to the education professionals to answer those questions. After all, he reasons, they are the experts.

As a consequence, MI-inspired pedagogy has been a grass-roots movement from its inception. Teachers have responded enthusiastically to the potential of this new model for instruction. Yet the ramifications go much further than we may realize. You can't tout the legitimacy of Gardner's work and in the same breath ask if there is a prepackaged MI curriculum or a series of MI volumes containing reproducible activity sheets. If you do, you are missing the far-reaching implications of Gardner's model. If multiple intelligences exist, then all bets are off on everything that we think of as "standardized" in education. If multiple intelligences exist, then we need to find a new model for teaching and measuring student mastery.

Formative and Summative Assessments

Because learning is an ongoing process, both formative and summative methods of assessment must take place when addressing multiple intelligences through technology. Formative assessments are snapshots in time that allow teachers and students to check on progress in the process of learning. Formative assessments are ongoing and provide information that allows the teacher to modify instruction to increase opportunities for student success. For example, Mr. Houghton may start out with the stated objective "mastery of long-division," but when he realizes students are still struggling with the two-digit multiplication algorithm, he revises his plan to revisit the process and strengthen his students' skills before proceeding with his original objective. In this way, formative assessment and instruction form a continuous cycle that fuels itself (Figure 9).

FIGURE 9
Cycle of Formative Assessment and Instruction

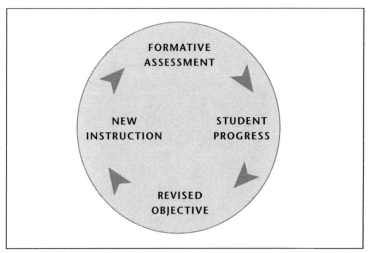

Summative assessments, on the other hand, are measures of student success at the completion of a lesson or unit. They require students to take skills and concepts and apply them at higher levels of thinking. For this reason, traditional paper and pencil assessments have used essays, word problems, and lengthy objective sections to measure the degree to which students have truly mastered material. Traditionally, summative assessments have been very final in the way they have been implemented. Once the test on Civil War Reconstruction is given before spring break, for example, it typically indicates that this chapter in history is over for this school year. What if those summative assessment scores were used to help determine the next unit of instruction, though? Couldn't the summative assessment cycle also be used in planning for new instruction?

Summative assessment is an important piece of the teaching puzzle. Accurately measuring what you've taught to find out what students have actually mastered and to what degree is vital if you intend to build on previous instruction with new skills and content. After all, if you haven't taught logarithms with a graphing calculator successfully, what's the point of moving on to quadratic equations? The question becomes: *How* do we best conduct our summative assessment? Do we use strictly paper and pencil assessments, and if so, why? We know that students with a strong kinesthetic or visual intelligence can master quadratic equations, but we also know that they will need to conceptualize and analyze them differently from those students possessing a strong logical intelligence. Is your classroom a sink or swim experience, or do your students all rise with the water level as they find their own effective ways to stay afloat?

Making Good Assessment Choices

Consider the role assessment plays in a computer lab through the choices of two second-grade teachers who are both responsible for science standards on life cycles, metamorphosis, and animal migration.

Teacher A always makes sure she is in the lab for her allotted computer time. She quickly gets her students on the machines to draw and paint pictures of butterflies while she sits at an empty counter madly grading papers. When the 45 minutes are up, the kids can say they've had their computer time, and they love the idea of spending three-quarters of an hour drawing. This teacher has had no interaction with her students, and she has assumed that they will see the connection between their classroom study of butterfly migration and this unstructured lab time.

Teacher B also always makes sure she has her class in the computer lab on time. She uses the projector at the demonstration station to guide her class through a virtual tracking of monarch butterflies migrating from the northeastern United States to Central America. All students are on task and following her lead as they discover the majesty of one of nature's most impressive annual treks. When students have questions or concerns, she is able to address them promptly, and before lab time is over she has each student working on a monarch butterfly scavenger hunt she uploaded to the school Web site weeks before. As they work on their hunt, she is free to move around the lab and interact with students as they apply what they know about the monarch. Teacher B will use the results of each child's hunt to determine where she will go in her science instruction for the next six weeks.

Which students understood the goal of their lab lesson? Which teacher addresses more intelligences in her classroom? Which teacher will have more success when it comes time for the state standardized tests?

Some teachers will counter: "But what about those standardized tests? If I have my students learning cooperatively and completing all kinds of projects all year, they'll never be ready for those state tests." The next time you hear that argument, remember my student Jamie and the incredible academic achievements he made in his fourth-grade year with less traditional instruction and assessment. Forcing children to complete pencil and paper tasks all year will not make them any more prepared to successfully complete standardized tests according to their abilities. Rather, I would argue that children with lots of concrete experiences and higher level applications of the curriculum will fare *better* on standardized tests than students taught traditionally.

Good test takers aren't successful because they know all the content by heart. They're good test takers because they can infer and deduce information and make correct choices a high percentage of the time. Memorizing facts may suffice for a multiple-choice test, but any master teacher will tell you that students really haven't mastered a skill or concept until they can apply it in a completely novel context. For example, any standardized test can ask a student to identify the major organs in the digestive system of a fetal pig, but the student who is able to take that working knowledge and identify similar organs while manually dissecting the feline digestive system demonstrates true mastery of this knowledge. Which student would you rather have working in your laboratory? Gardner's definition of intelligence resounds clearly: the ability to create products and solve problems that are of value in one's own culture. This is the essence of authentic assessment: to demonstrate understanding through the accomplishment of rich, real-world, performance-based tasks. When all students can demonstrate these abilities in math, science, history, language, and the arts, then we will have truly revolutionized public education.

Having said all this, what kinds of assessment should we be using? Authentic assessments, certainly, but do we need to provide an authentic assessment for every skill that matches every intelligence in the classroom? Thankfully, no. Just as no one lesson should attempt to cover all the intelligences, neither should one assessment. Rather, plan your assessments globally so that in the course of any unit or project students will get the opportunity to perform assessments that will stimulate all the intelligences. This serves a twofold purpose. First, students will have a chance to demonstrate their mastery regardless of their strengths. And second, they will be exposed to all kinds of tasks so that they have the opportunity to strengthen those intelligences that are not already well developed.

The OPP Chart

An excellent way to develop a sound authentic assessment task is to use an OPP chart (Objective, Procedure, Product). An OPP chart requires teachers to refer to the original objective in a lesson, examine how well the objective is taught through the procedure of the lesson, and then identify a product that demonstrates the degree of student mastery. Consider the process of developing an OPP chart for a third-grade social studies lesson.

Objective

Given graph paper, pencil, ruler, and markers, the learner will create a map of the classroom that includes a legend with symbols for doorways, windows, counters, closets, and furniture.

Procedure

1 Examine a variety of maps and review their features (grid, legend, compass rose).

2 Create a wall-sized mock-up sketch of the classroom with student input to help encourage thinking about everything that should be included in a map of the classroom.

3 Have students work in pairs to map the classroom accurately with a legend for doorways, windows, counters, closets, and furniture.

Product

Completed classroom maps will be evaluated for neatness and accurate placement of doorways, windows, counters, closets, and furniture.

The OPP chart for this lesson looks like Table 31.

TABLE 31

OPP Chart for a Third-Grade Social Studies Lesson		
OPP	**INTELLIGENCES**	**BLOOM**
Objective Create maps on graph paper with a legend of symbols for doorways, windows, counters, closets, and furniture.	Visual Naturalist	Synthesis
Procedure Brainstorm map elements and then have students work in pairs to create original classroom maps.	Visual Naturalist	Synthesis
Product Classroom maps that are evaluated for neatness and accuracy.	Logical	Comprehension

This is a very well-intentioned lesson. Students are being asked to apply their knowledge of mapping to create original maps that make use of a symbol system to denote major objects in the classroom. However, have another look at the OPP chart in Table 31. The objective stresses use of symbols in a legend, but the product is being evaluated for neatness and accuracy. The objective emphasizes the visual and naturalist intelligences, but the product is examined for use of the logical intelligence. Finally, the objective asks students to work at Bloom's synthesis level, but the evaluation is much lower on the taxonomy. There is a clear mismatch between objective and evaluation. Perhaps the objective can be reworded to stress neatness and accuracy, or perhaps evaluation of the product can be modified to emphasize the symbols in the legend rather than a clean, precise classroom map. Whatever choice the teacher makes, the goal will be to line up this OPP chart so there is agreement all the way through.

Table 32 shows another example. This seventh-grade English teacher is going to teach the soliloquy form as part of his study of *The Merchant of Venice.*

TABLE 32

OPP Chart for *The Merchant of Venice* Soliloquy Lesson		
OPP	**INTELLIGENCES**	**BLOOM**
Objective Analyze the elements of a Shakespearean soliloquy, including rhyme, meter, and content.	Musical Verbal Logical	Application and analysis
Procedure Study the form and content of a soliloquy from *The Merchant of Venice* as an example.	Musical Verbal Logical	Application and analysis
Product Recite the soliloquy from *The Merchant of Venice* from memory.	Musical Verbal Logical	Knowledge

This is a classic lesson we all have encountered at some point in our education. It is well intended and it is surely laudable to have students study, memorize, and recite a soliloquy as part of their study of Shakespeare. Still, look at the OPP chart. The objective starts out as a direct, succinct, measurable goal. It emphasizes the musical, verbal, and logical intelligences. In the procedure, students immerse themselves in a specific soliloquy and learn to appreciate the genre. It follows the objective nicely. However, look at the product. Does recitation of a dozen lines from Shakespeare demonstrate an understanding of the form and content of the soliloquy? While the objective clearly calls for application and analysis, simple recitation has students functioning at the knowledge level of Bloom's taxonomy. To make this an effective lesson, this assessment will have to be completely rewritten, as in Table 33.

TABLE 33

Revised OPP Chart for *The Merchant of Venice* Soliloquy Lesson		
OPP	**INTELLIGENCES**	**BLOOM**
Objective Analyze the elements of a Shakespearean soliloquy, including rhyme, meter, and content.	Musical Verbal Logical	Application and analysis
Procedure Study the form and content of a soliloquy from *The Merchant of Venice* as an example.	Musical Verbal Logical	Application and analysis
Product Analyze a second Shakespearean soliloquy and contrast the two soliloquies in terms of rhyme, meter, and content.	Musical Verbal Logical	Application and analysis

Now this lesson consistently targets the objective and the musical, verbal, and logical intelligences from start to finish. The OPP chart is an effective way to line up your assessment tasks so that you can accurately measure the learning that takes place in your classroom.

As a final example, Table 34 shows a lesson Aimee Smith uses with her Algebra 1 and 2 students, called the Cube Problem. She has provided a detailed scoring rubric for assessment at the end of the lesson.

TABLE 34

Cube Problem Lesson

LESSON TITLE: Cube Problem
TEACHER: Aimee Smith, Urbana High School, Urbana, Illinois
GRADE LEVEL: 9
SUBJECT(S): Math   **TIME FRAME:** 3 class periods

OBJECTIVE(S)	INTELLIGENCES	TECHNOLOGIES	STANDARDS
• To apply math concepts to a real-world problem. • To work in groups to determine a solution and present it to the class.		Microsoft Office Internet Browser	**NETS for Students:** **3. Technology productivity tools** • Students use technology tools to enhance learning, increase productivity, and promote creativity.

(Continued)

Cube Problem Lesson

(Continued)

OBJECTIVE(S)	INTELLIGENCES	TECHNOLOGIES	STANDARDS
			3. **Technology productivity tools** • Students use productivity tools to collaborate in constructing technology-enhanced models, preparing publications, and producing other creative works. 6. **Technology problem-solving and decision-making tools** • Students use technology resources for solving problems and making informed decisions. • Students employ technology in the development of strategies for solving problems in the real world.

MATERIALS	INTELLIGENCES
Cube Problem Handout Computers Internet Access Microsoft Office	

PROCEDURE

Timeline
Day 1: Students work on the cube problem in groups in class.
Day 2: Cube problem presentations begin. (Students prepare for presentations during the first half of the period, and begin giving presentations during the second half of the period.)
Day 3: Students finish giving cube problem presentations. The teacher explains the cube report and its due date.

Activities
Present students with the following scenario: You plan to start a small business making black plywood cubes that can be used as end tables or plant stands. Each cube is 18 inches long on each edge. Your problem is to determine how much you should charge for each cube.

(Continued)

Cube Problem Lesson

(Continued)

PROCEDURE	INTELLIGENCES
Students are given the following information: • The plywood to make one cube costs $7.50. • The nails and glue for 100 cubes cost $25.00. • The paint and lacquer for 100 cubes cost $75.00. • Assemblers make $6.00 per hour. One worker can assemble 3 cubes in 1 hour. • Painters make $8.00 per hour. One worker can paint 5 cubes in 1 hour. • Plastic wrapping to protect the cubes during shipping costs $0.65 per cube. In groups, students must first determine the cost to manufacture one cube, and then decide how much to charge for each cube. A good rule of thumb for pricing manufactured items is to double the cost of manufacture. In groups, students will present their solution and work to the class. To do this they may choose to use as visual aids a large whiteboard and dry erase markers, white butcher paper and markers, or the overhead projector and transparencies.	

PRODUCT	
Students will write a report recommending the amount to be charged for each cube. Students should include a complete explanation of how they arrived at this conclusion. This report should be typed and may include a picture if necessary.	

ASSESSMENT	
See Table 35, Grading Criteria for Cube Problem Lesson.	

TABLE 35

Grading Criteria for Cube Problem Lesson

Cube Problem—Group Tasks

Each item will be assessed out of 2 points, for a total of 16 points.
(⓪ points = poor, ① point = good, ② points = excellent.)

Group members: _____

Individual Responsibilities (as part of my group) I am responsible for...				*Team Responsibilities* We are responsible for...			
Trying. Improvement counts!	⓪	①	②	*Solving.* We try to solve our own problems.	⓪	①	②
Asking. Ask for help from teammates.	⓪	①	②	*Asking Team Questions.* We ask teammates			
Helping. Offer help to teammates.	⓪	①	②	before asking the teacher.	⓪	①	②
Courtesy. Make polite requests and				*Helping.* We help other teams, classmates,			
show appreciation.	⓪	①	②	and the teacher.	⓪	①	②
				Modulated Voice. We use a voice heard			
				by teammates, but not other teams.	⓪	①	②

Group Tasks Grade: _____ / 16 points

(Continued)

Grading Criteria for Cube Problem Lesson

(Continued)

Cube Problem—Presentation

Date: _____

(Each section will be assessed out of 5 points, for a total of 20 points.)

Presentation Techniques
Organization
Neatness
Use of media
Oral skills
Good visualization
① ② ③ ④ ⑤

Correctness of Answers
Process
Accuracy
Knowledge
Ability to answer questions
① ② ③ ④ ⑤

Completeness (as assigned)
Problem awareness
Facts
Math concepts
① ② ③ ④ ⑤

Participation
Involved
Team oriented
All have a part in the presentation
① ② ③ ④ ⑤

Presentation Grade: _____ / 20 points

Cube Problem—Report

Assignment
Write a report recommending how much you should charge for each cube.

Length
Between half a page and one full page.

Grading
5 points for the correct math content.
   • Make sure you explain how you came up with your numbers.
10 points for your explanation for how you arrived at your answer.
   • Be thorough and detailed.
   • Pretend you are explaining how you solved the problem to someone who has no previous knowledge of the situation.
5 points for neatness and organization.
   • You may type it or hand write it, but I must be able to read it.

Report Grade: _____ / 20 points

Remarks:

How would you assess the work of Aimee's students? Use an OPP chart to determine which intelligences and Bloom levels should be targeted. Which strategies would help you assess the process as well as the product for Aimee's students?

If it all comes down to assessment, then the way you assess authentic tasks is extremely important. In constructing authentic assessments, devise open-ended tasks that allow each student to apply the skills and concepts you have taught in novel ways, much like Aimee does in her Cube Problem. Do you want to assess students' understanding of the causes of the American Revolution? Ask each student to create a presentation of the colonists' grievances against the King with at least seven specific references to actual events that occurred between 1763 and 1775. Evaluating a class's knowledge of how sound waves travel? Ask students to create their own experiments that demonstrate how to lengthen and shorten sound waves so that one can tell aurally what is happening to the sound. Time to assess student mastery of measuring mass? Have them construct balsa wood balance scales that can weigh up to 2 pounds accurately.

The possibilities are all around you. It simply requires each of us to look at assessment with a different point of reference than the way we ourselves were taught.

Rubric Construction

One excellent authentic assessment tool is the rubric. Rubrics provide quantitative evaluation of student work while offering qualitative feedback. Teachers have the standards for students in place, and students can expect input that will help them understand how their work measures up against those standards *and* what they can do to improve their performance. It's a win-win situation.

Here are some suggestions for constructing rubrics:

- Use student input in creating standards for the rubric.

- Create the rubric using a spreadsheet template so that it is easy to fill in, calculate, and save.

- Identify the intelligences you are using for each criterion on your rubric. This will help you determine whether your assessment addresses the same intelligences your objectives intended.

- Use highly descriptive indicators for degrees of success and include numerical weights so students can see differentiated levels of success.

- Present the rubric to students before they begin their task so that they keep in mind the criteria for completing the task successfully.

- Have students complete the rubric on their own work in progress, then share their perceptions with you before you complete the rubric on their product.

For example, using the authentic task "In a clean, easy-to-follow format, create a presentation that states the colonists' grievances against the King with at least seven specific references to actual events that occurred between 1763 and 1775," the rubric may look like that in Table 36.

TABLE 36

American Revolution Rubric

	Unsatisfactory ①	Satisfactory ②	Excellent ③	Total
Selected an effective medium to complete the task. (Visual)	Presentation did not display grievances.	Presentation displayed grievances.	Presentation displayed grievances in a compelling, forceful way.	
Created presentation in a clean, easy-to-follow format. (Verbal)	Presentation was messy and hard to read or understand.	Presentation was clean, neat, and easy to follow.	Presentation was clean, neat, and easy to follow, and provided a greater understanding of the grievances.	
Included 7 or more events that occurred between 1763 and 1775. (Logical)	Presentation contained fewer than 7 events or contained fictional events.	Presentation included 7 actual historic events.	Presentation included more than 7 actual historic events.	
Explained how each event was a justified grievance from the colonists' point of view. (Intrapersonal)	Presentation listed events without explaining their effect on colonists.	Presentation explained how each event was a justified grievance from the colonists' point of view.	Presentation explained how each event was a justified grievance and showed how each event built on previous resentments.	
Presented the final product to the class successfully. (Interpersonal)	Student presented a final product that was incomplete or inaccurate.	Student presented a final product that successfully explained the colonists' grievances.	Student presented a final product that successfully explained the colonists' grievances and successfully answered audience questions on the subject.	

SCALE

13–15   Student shows excellent mastery of the causes of the American Revolution.

10–12   Student shows sufficient mastery of the causes of the American Revolution.

0–9   Student does not show mastery of the causes of the American Revolution.

With this rubric, the student can score a maximum of 15 points. The teacher has already determined that a score of 10 or higher is needed to pass the assessment, and that a score of 9 or lower indicates that the student has not mastered an understanding of the causes of the American Revolution. Is there any doubt that after completing this assessment both the student and teacher will know to what degree the causes of the American Revolution have been mastered in the classroom? Is there any question that students who perform at the Excellent level of the rubric will do well on questions on the causes of the American Revolution that appear on a standardized test? A well-constructed rubric is a strong teaching and assessment tool.

Consider the lesson in Table 37, especially the assessment strategies at the end of the lesson (Table 38, Table 39, and Table 40). This lesson was presented by Gary Ribis to his high school students. Note how he builds in flexibility in his grading and how he collects multiple forms of data on student performance.

TABLE 37

Seeing the Forest... and the Trees! Lesson

LESSON TITLE: Seeing the Forest... and the Trees!
TEACHER: Gary Ribis, Long Beach High School, Long Beach, New York
GRADE LEVEL: 6–8
SUBJECT(S): Science (Ecology)   **TIME FRAME:** 2 weeks

OBJECTIVE(S)	INTELLIGENCES	TECHNOLOGIES	STANDARDS
• Record names of trees.	Verbal	Word processor	**NETS for Students:**
• Use trees as inspiration in various creative tasks.	Logical	Calculator	**2. Social, ethical, and human issues** • Students develop positive attitudes toward technology uses that support lifelong learning, collaboration, personal pursuits, and productivity.
• Draw the cellular structure of a tree root.	Naturalist		
• Chart the growth of a tree.	Visual	Draw or paint software	
• Learn how trees contribute to the ecosystem.	Kinesthetic		**5. Technology research tools** • Students use technology to locate, evaluate, and collect information from a variety of sources.
• Learn about the scientific method for classifying plant life.	Logical Musical	Database or spreadsheet software	

(Continued)

Seeing the Forest... and the Trees! Lesson

(Continued)

OBJECTIVE(S)	INTELLIGENCES	TECHNOLOGIES	STANDARDS
			6. Technology problem-solving and decision-making tools • Students use technology resources for solving problems and making informed decisions.

MATERIALS	INTELLIGENCES
Leaf and bark samples of local trees	Kinesthetic
Leaf classification charts and handouts	Naturalist
Overhead projections	Visual
Rulers (standard and metric)	Logical
Paper and colored pencils/other drawing utensils	Visual
Clay	Kinesthetic
Computer	
Biology textbook	Visual
Web sites: http://enloehs.wcpss.net/science/warner/Rainforest/page.htm http://enloehs.wcpss.net/science/warner/Forest/titlepage.htm www.rainbird.com/rainforest/download.htm www.rainbird.com/pdf/rainforest/rainbird_9-12.pdf www.marietta.edu/~biol/102/grasslnd.html www.thescienceconnection.net/environmentalbiomes/	

PROCEDURE

	INTELLIGENCES
Give your class the following instructions: You'll soon be on your way to learning more about the trees in our environment. Here's a way to start becoming experts. The tasks listed below will require the participation and strengths of everyone in your group. After completing Task Cards 1–6, your group will develop an oral PowerPoint presentation (Task Card 7).	
Task Card 1 Draw the cellular structure of a tree root.	Visual Kinesthetic
Task Card 2 Determine the most popular tree in class by interviewing others.	Verbal Intrapersonal
Task Card 3 Create different parts of a tree from clay.	Visual Kinesthetic

(Continued)

Seeing the Forest... and the Trees! Lesson

(Continued)

PROCEDURE	INTELLIGENCES
Task Card 4 Create a poem or tree song based on information in this unit. Your song or poem should be at least 10 lines long.	Verbal Musical
Task Card 5 Given weather, soil, and other information, chart the projected growth of a tree. Use the computer to publish your graph. Include a title and labels.	Logical Musical Naturalist
Task Card 6 Explain how a tree functions in relation to the ecosystem. Record this information for use in your PowerPoint presentation.	Naturalist Existential
Task Card 7 Have each group member choose a leaf from a particular tree. Create a classification system for the leaves, then develop a PowerPoint presentation that describes the leaves and their classification. Be prepared to present your leaves and classification system to the class using PowerPoint.	Logical Naturalist Visual Verbal Interpersonal

PRODUCT	
Group PowerPoint presentation	Verbal Visual Logical Intrapersonal Interpersonal Naturalist Existential

ASSESSMENT	
Quizzes and tests, plus peer evaluation, cooperative group and PowerPoint rubrics.	Verbal Visual Logical Intrapersonal Interpersonal

Assessment Strategies

The following rubrics have been developed to evaluate the Seeing the Forest... and the Trees! lesson:

Table 38. PowerPoint Rubric

Table 39. Cooperative Group Rubric

Table 40. Peer Evaluation Rubric for Oral Presentation

TABLE 38

PowerPoint Rubric

	Exemplary	Proficient	Partially Proficient	Incomplete
Research and Note-taking	**6 points** Note cards show group members recorded relevant information from many varied sources. Students thoughtfully and correctly interpreted and synthesized statements, graphics, and questions, and evaluated alternative points of view.	**4 points** Note cards show group members recorded relevant information from multiple sources. Students correctly interpreted and synthesized statements, graphics, and questions, and evaluated alternative points of view.	**2 points** Note cards show group members recorded information from at least five sources. Students misinterpreted statements, graphics, and questions, and on many occasions failed to note alternative points of view.	**0 points** Note cards show group members recorded information from four or fewer sources. Students misinterpreted statements, graphics, and questions, and ignored alternative points of view.
Preproduction Plan— Storyboard	**6 points** The storyboard has a balanced number of thumbnail sketches. They are numbered and in a logical sequence. Each slide includes a title and text; a background color; good placement and size of graphic elements; attention to font color, font size, and font type for text and headings; hyperlinks (listing URLs of any site linked from the slide); and other practical and creative elements.	**4 points** The storyboard has an adequate number of thumbnail sketches. They are in a logical sequence, and titles and text are provided for each slide. Some additional practical and creative elements are included.	**2 points** The storyboard has only a few thumbnail sketches. They are not in a logical sequence, and titles and text are incomplete.	**0 points** The storyboard has very few thumbnail sketches. They are not in a logical sequence, and titles and text are missing.

(Continued)

PowerPoint Rubric

(Continued)

	Exemplary	Proficient	Partially Proficient	Incomplete
Introduction	**3 points** The introduction provides a clear, logical orientation. It presents the overall topic well and draws the audience into the presentation with compelling questions or by relating to the audience's interests or goals.	**2 points** The introduction provides a clear, logical orientation. It is concise and coherent, and appealing to the audience.	**1 point** The introduction shows some structure but does not create a strong sense of what will follow. It may be overly detailed or incomplete and is somewhat appealing to the audience.	**0 points** The introduction does not orient the audience to what will follow. The sequencing is unclear and is not interesting or relevant to the audience.
Content	**8 points** The content demonstrates a logical, thoughtful progression of ideas. Supporting information is strong, and the point of view is clear and concise. The project includes persuasive information and motivating questions that provide the audience with a strong sense of the project's main idea. Many relevant facts are included. Information is accurate and current. Primary sources have been tapped for most information.	**6 points** The content demonstrates a logical progression of ideas. Supporting information is sufficient, and the point of view is clear. The project includes persuasive information with several relevant facts. Information is accurate and somewhat current. Primary sources have been tapped for some information.	**4 points** The content somewhat lacks a logical progression of ideas. Supporting information is insufficient, and the point of view is vague. The project includes some persuasive information with a few relevant facts. Information may not be accurate or current. Some of it does not seem to fit. Primary source use is not always clear.	**0 points** The content lacks a logical progression of ideas. Supporting information is missing, and there is no clear point of view. The project includes little persuasive information and only one or two relevant facts. Information may be inaccurate, out of date, unrelated, or incomplete. Primary sources have not been used.

(Continued)

PowerPoint Rubric

(Continued)

	Exemplary	Proficient	Partially Proficient	Incomplete
Text Elements	**3 points** The text is easy to read. The point size is appealing and varies appropriately for headings and body text. The use of harmonious fonts, italics, bold, color, and pleasing backgrounds enhances readability. Paragraphs are the appropriate length. Indentations are well used and appealing.	**2 points** The text is sometimes easy to read. The point size is somewhat appropriate but unbalanced in places. In a few places the use of unusual fonts, italics, bold, color, and busy backgrounds detracts from readability. Some paragraphs may be too long. Indentations may not be used well.	**1 point** The text is difficult to read. The point size is too small or too large and unbalanced. There are too many different fonts, the use of italics and bold is inappropriate, the color choices are poor, and the backgrounds are dark or busy. Paragraphs are too long. Indentations are inappropriate.	**0 points** The text is extremely difficult to read. The point size is too small or too large and unbalanced. There are too many different fonts, the use of italics and bold is inappropriate, the color choices are poor, and the backgrounds are dark or busy. The overall effect is unappealing. Paragraphs are too long. Indentations are inappropriate.
Layout	**3 points** The layout is structured and aesthetically pleasing. It contributes to the overall message with the appropriate and appealing use of headings, subheadings, and white space.	**2 points** The layout is structured and somewhat clear. Headings and subheadings are arranged appropriately, and the use of white space is appealing.	**1 point** The layout shows some structure, but appears cluttered and busy. Headings and subheadings are arranged haphazardly, and large gaps of white space or crowded areas are distracting.	**0 points** The layout is without structure, cluttered, and confusing. The use of headings, subheadings, and white space does not enhance the readability.
Citations	**6 points** All sources are documented so that the accuracy, credibility, and authority of the information can be checked. All sources are properly cited using the MLA format.	**4 points** Most sources are documented so that the accuracy, credibility, and authority of the information can be checked. Most sources are properly cited using the MLA format.	**2 points** Some sources are documented so that the accuracy, credibility, and authority of the information can be checked. Some sources are properly cited using the MLA format.	**0 points** None of the sources are documented so that the accuracy, credibility, and authority of the information can be checked. None of the sources are properly cited using the MLA format.

(Continued)

PowerPoint Rubric

(Continued)

	Exemplary	Proficient	Partially Proficient	Incomplete
Graphics, Sound, or Animations	**3 points** The graphics, sound, or animations are related to the topic and interwoven seamlessly. They provide visual connections that enhance the understanding of the content.	**2 points** The graphics, sound, or animations are related to the topic. They are appealing and enhance the understanding of the content.	**1 point** Some of the graphics, sounds, or animations are unrelated to the topic. They do little to enhance the understanding of the content.	**0 points** The graphics, sounds, or animations are unrelated to the topic. They do not enhance the understanding of the content, or they create a busy feeling and detract from the content.
	All images are original.	Most images are original.	Most images are clip art or recycled from the WWW.	All images are clip art or recycled from the WWW.
	Images are the proper size, are nicely cropped, and have a clear resolution.	Images are mostly the proper size, are nicely cropped, and have a somewhat clear resolution.	Images are too large or too small. They are poorly cropped, and the resolution is fuzzy.	Images are too large or too small. They are poorly cropped, and the resolution is fuzzy.
Writing Mechanics	**6 points** The text has no errors in grammar, capitalization, punctuation, spelling, or usage.	**4 points** The text has one or two errors in grammar, capitalization, punctuation, spelling, or usage.	**2 points** The text has three to five errors in grammar, capitalization, punctuation, spelling, or usage.	**0 points** The text has more than five errors in grammar, capitalization, punctuation, spelling, or usage.
	No editing is required.	Little or no editing is required.	Some editing is required.	Major editing is required.
Teamwork	**6 points** The group did not require teacher assistance in dividing tasks or resolving differences.	**4 points** The group required little teacher assistance in dividing tasks or resolving differences.	**2 points** The group occasionally helped one another but required teacher assistance in dividing tasks and resolving differences.	**0 points** The group required teacher assistance in dividing tasks and resolving differences.
	The group documents how members shared the workload, were supportive, and managed problems in a way that advanced the group goal. The project is clearly a group effort.	The group documents how members shared the workload and managed problems in a way that advanced the group goal.	One person documents that he or she did most of the work or that problems were not managed in a way that advanced the group goal.	Few people contributed their fair share of work.

TABLE 39

Cooperative Group Rubric

	Exemplary 4	Focused 3	Developing 2	Beginning 1
Contribution to Group				
Meets Deadlines	Hands in all assignments on time.	Hands in most assignments on time.	Hands in many assignments late.	Doesn't hand in assignments.
Contributes Information	Contributes a good deal of relevant information.	Contributes information that is somewhat relevant.	Contributes little information.	Does not contribute information.
Shares Information	Shares all information with the group.	Shares important information with the group.	Shares some information with the group.	Keeps information to self and doesn't share with the group.
Cooperation Within Group				
Cooperates With Group Members	Always cooperates.	Usually cooperates.	Seldom cooperates.	Never cooperates.
Listens to Group Members	Balances listening and speaking well.	Talks too much at times but is usually a good listener.	Talks much of the time and rarely allows others to speak.	Is always talking and never allows others to speak.
Makes Fair Decisions	Is a total team player.	Usually considers all viewpoints.	Often sides with friends and doesn't consider all viewpoints.	Always wants things his or her way.
Responsibility to Group				
Fulfills Duties	Performs all duties.	Performs nearly all duties.	Performs very few duties.	Does not perform any duties.
Shares Responsibility	Always does the work without being reminded.	Usually does the work and seldom needs reminding.	Rarely does the work and needs constant reminding.	Always relies on others to do the work.

TABLE 40

Peer Evaluation Rubric for Oral Presentation			
	Very Good 3	**Satisfactory** 2	**Poor** 1
Gave an interesting introduction			
Presented a clear explanation of the topic			
Presented information in an acceptable order			
Used complete sentences			
Offered a concluding summary			
Spoke clearly, correctly, distinctly, and confidently			
Maintained eye contact			
Maintained acceptable posture			
Offered an interesting presentation			
Used visual and audio aids well			
Handled questions and comments from the class well			

Is there any doubt that Gary will collect a rich set of data on each student's work in this lesson? It is data that will allow him not only to assess student learning, but also plan for ongoing instruction that builds on what he finds. Well-developed rubrics are an excellent form of student assessment.

Transforming the Classroom

Digital technology can play an important role in authentic assessment. So many productivity tools on the computer offer great presentation formats for culminating products. Slideshows, spreadsheets with charts and graphs, and Web sites are all effective ways to show student mastery of content that cannot be demonstrated as easily through other means. Imagine a presentation of the Civil Rights movement in PowerPoint, a spreadsheet chart with data on immigration statistics from 1820 to 1860, or an interactive periodic table of the elements on a student-created Web page in which each element's properties are linked to further information. Creating your rubric in a spreadsheet will allow you to include a digital assessment of student work to accompany their digital products. Welcome to the Information Age!

Regardless of the task, whether it is done on the computer, in hard copy, or as a performance, capture it digitally by using a digital camera or scanner so that you have a digital record of the student product to go along with the digital rubric. Where will you put all these digital artifacts? Why, in a digital portfolio, of course! Digital portfolios allow you to collect samples of authentic assessment tasks over time as well as the rubrics you use to assess them. They open up all kinds of possibilities for authentic assessment tasks that challenge students to solve problems and create products to demonstrate learning. You can set up individual student folders on floppy disks, on a computer hard drive, on a network server, or even on the Internet. With password protection for each folder, you can keep track of student work throughout the year without those bulky manila folders cluttering up drawers of your filing cabinet. Digital portfolios are compact, easy to retrieve, and always easy to modify as you see the need.

Consider the full potential of digital portfolios: they can be housed on your school server or in a protected virtual environment such as Blackboard or Yahoo Groups. Parents can be given their child's portfolio password so that they can view their child's progress from any Internet-connected computer 24 hours a day, 7 days a week. Add an e-mail link, and parents will be able to touch base with you whenever the need arises. It's the beginning of your own virtual classroom!

Still, all these wonderful possibilities are technotraditionalist in nature. We are trying to accomplish traditional tasks using digital tools: rubrics, work samples, portfolios. Eventually I foresee technoconstructivist educators who dare to transform the basic *formats* of the assessments they use. Imagine standardized tests in which students participate in virtual simulations, respond to stimuli, and solve problems within the context of real-world situations. Instead of filling in bubbles by selecting the letter that corresponds to a multiple-choice answer, students are at a computer interacting with a generative software application that provides stimuli and records student responses: a virtual canoe trip down a state scenic river, a digital science experiment in which the student controls the process, or a Shakespearean soliloquy that takes place against the backdrop of the Globe theater. The tests will still be norm-referenced and evaluated for validity and reliability, but students will have so many more opportunities to apply their knowledge and show their learning through all the different intelligences. Technology is the vehicle that MI can use to transport education into the future.

For all the possibilities, it is important to remember that there is no one set way to address the implications of MI for instruction. Rather, we should be focused on keeping the doors of education open to allow for all the things that can happen when these powerful movements in education are allowed to realize their potential. Your students' intelligences will flourish when you offer open-ended tasks that allow multiple points of entry and response. MI theory is not meant to be a set of labels or categories for teachers to keep record of. The intelligences always function in your classroom at some level, whether you acknowledge them or not!

As for that classroom of the future where students can demonstrate their mastery of content regardless of how their intelligences are distributed, it's not as far away as we think. State departments of education are already moving toward automated standardized testing. Once that is accomplished, test formats dictated by the limitations of pencil and paper will give way to the possibilities discussed in this book. Dr. Gardner has asked questions that must be answered, and technology is leading the way. What an exciting time to be in education!

Resources for Further Study

Print

Arter, J., & McTighe, J. (2000). *Scoring rubrics in the classroom: Using performance criteria for assessing and improving student performance.* Thousand Oaks, CA: Corwin Press.

Baron, C. (2003). *Designing a digital portfolio.* Berkeley, CA: New Riders Press.

Gura, M., & Reissman, R. (Eds.). (2001). *Making literacy magic happen: The best of* Learning & Leading with Technology *on language arts.* Eugene, OR: International Society for Technology in Education.

Hassard, J. (1999). *Science as inquiry: Active learning, project-based, Web-assisted, and active assessment strategies to enhance student learning.* Tucson, AZ: GoodYear Books.

NETS Project. (2003). *National educational technology standards for teachers: Resources for assessment.* Eugene, OR: International Society for Technology in Education.

Stevens, D. D., & Levi, A. J. (2004). *Introduction to rubrics: An assessment tool to save grading time, convey effective feedback and promote student learning.* Sterling, VA: Stylus.

Teich, A. H. (2002). *Technology and the future.* Florence, KY: Wadsworth.

Online

Assessment Tools:
www.tcet.unt.edu/START/assess/tools.htm

Getting Started With Digital Portfolios:
www.essentialschools.org/pub/ces_docs/resources/dp/getstart.html

Practical Assessment, Research & Evaluation:
http://pareonline.net

Rubistar:
http://rubistar.4teachers.org/index.php

Secondary Assessment Tools:
ww.bcpl.net/%7Esullivan/modules/tips/assess_sec.html

6 + 1 Trait Analytical Assessment Model:
www.nwrel.org/assessment/department.asp?d=1

Teacher Rubric Makers:
www.teach-nology.com/web_tools/rubrics/

Reflections

1 How do your assessment strategies dictate the kinds of instructional strategies you choose?

2 Create a rubric for a lesson presented earlier in the text using the template provided on the accompanying CD-ROM. What did you find easy in creating this rubric? What did you find difficult?

3 Would digital student portfolios encourage you to include technology more frequently in your instruction?

4 How do you envision technoconstructivist assessment formats?

Multiple Intelligences Survey for Older Students

Multiple Intelligences Survey for Older Students

For each statement, enter a number one (1) if you agree with the statement or enjoy the activity being described. Enter a number zero (0) if you do not.

I LIKE...		I LIKE...	
Sorting things into groups.		Chatting online.	
Thinking about life.		Having strong feelings about things.	
Picturing things in my mind.		Playing sports.	
Working with my hands.		Studying religion.	
Studying patterns.		Making art.	
Keeping things in order.		Moving to a beat.	
Studying with a partner.		Writing stories.	
Looking at the big picture.		Solving problems.	
Learning a new language.		Completing a word-find puzzle.	
Being right.		Being on a team.	
Listening to sounds in nature.		Drawing maps.	
Moving around.		Hiking and camping.	
Making up nonsense words.		Playing an instrument.	
Following directions.		Practicing sign language.	
Protecting nature.		Studying art.	
Decorating a room.		Having things neat and tidy.	

(Continued)

Multiple Intelligences Survey for Older Students

I LIKE...		I LIKE...	
Studying different countries.		Working alone.	
Being fair.		Observing the stars and planets.	
Writing in a diary.		Using my imagination.	
Rhyming words.		Learning about animals.	
Watching a play.		Listening to all kinds of music.	
Working in a garden.		Using tools.	
Figuring out math problems.		Joining a club.	
Being a good friend.		Discussing world issues.	
Listening to music.		Being a leader.	
Talking on the phone.		Giving a speech.	
Wondering about the universe.		Marching to a beat.	
Exercising.		Knowing why I should do something.	
Visiting national parks.		Keeping things neat.	
Feeling good about my work.		Summarizing ideas.	
Remembering poems or words to songs.		Building things.	
Creating graphs and charts.		Recycling waste.	
Making timelines.		Taking notes.	
Having a debate.		Working with others.	
Getting along with others.		Planning things in my mind.	
Putting together a puzzle.		Wondering about life on other planets.	
Reading charts and tables.		Being treated fairly.	
Making arts and crafts.		Going to the zoo.	
Helping the poor.		Making lists.	
Being with other people.		Playing charades.	
Answering riddles.		Listening to a story.	
Watching a video.		Reading books.	
Writing letters.		Being around other people.	
Dancing.		Spending time outdoors.	
Having background noise while I work.		Sensing something is about to happen.	
Speaking up when I see something wrong.			

Multiple Intelligences
Survey for Younger Students

STUDENT NAME _____

Circle each picture that shows an activity you like to do.

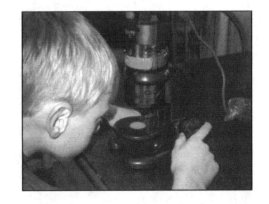

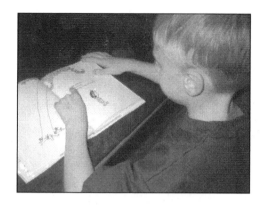

TOTALS

Verbal _____

Logical _____

Visual _____

Kinesthetic _____

Musical _____

Intrapersonal _____

Interpersonal _____

Naturalist _____

Existential _____

APPENDIX C

Bibliography

A

Armstrong, T. (2000). *Multiple intelligences in the classroom* (2nd ed.). Alexandria, VA: Association for Supervision and Curriculum Development.

Armstrong, T. (2003). *Multiple intelligences of reading and writing: Making the words come alive.* Alexandria, VA: Association for Supervision and Curriculum Development.

Asen, S. (1992). *Teaching and learning with technology.* Alexandria, VA: Association for Supervision and Curriculum Development.

Ayers, E. L., & Grisham, C. M. (November/December 2003). Why IT has not paid off as we hoped (yet). *Educause Review 38*(6), 40–51. Also available online at www.educause.edu/pub/er/erm03/erm0361.asp

B

Berger, R. (2003). *An ethic of excellence: Building a culture of craftsmanship with students.* London: Reed Elsevier.

C

Campbell, L., Campbell, B., & Dickinson, D. (2003). *Teaching and learning through multiple intelligences* (2nd ed.). Upper Saddle River, NJ: Allyn & Bacon.

F

Fuller, H. (Summer 2000). First teach their teachers: Technology support and computer use in academic subjects. *Journal of Research on Computing in Education, 32*(4), 511–537.

G

Gardner, H. (1983). *Frames of mind.* New York: Basic Books.

Gardner, H. (1991). *Multiple intelligences: Theory into practice.* New York: Basic Books.

Gardner, H. (1991). *The unschooled mind: How children think and how schools should teach.* New York: Basic Books.

Gardner, H. (1999). *The disciplined mind.* New York: Simon & Schuster.

Gardner, H. (1999). *Intelligence reframed.* New York: Basic Books.

Goleman, D. (1997). *Emotional intelligence.* New York: Bantam.

H

Harris, J. (1998). *Virtual architecture: Designing and directing curriculum-based telecomputing.* Eugene, OR: International Society for Technology in Education.

Hoerr, T. (2000). *Technology and MI.* Available online at www.newhorizons.org/strategies/mi/hoerr.htm

Hoerr, T. (2002). *Applying MI in schools.* Available online at www.newhorizons.org/strategies/mi/hoerr2.htm

Hopson, M. H., Simms, R. L., & Knezek, G. A. (Winter 2001–2002). Using a technology-enriched environment to improve higher-order thinking skills. *Journal of Research on Technology in Education, 34*(2), 109–119.

Howard, B. C., McGee, S., Schwartz, N., & Purcell, S. (Summer 2000). The experience of constructivism: Transforming teacher epistemology. *Journal of Research on Computing in Education, 32*(4), 455–465.

J

Jacobs, H. H. (1997). *Mapping the big picture: Integrating curriculum and assessment K–12.* Alexandria, VA: Association for Supervision and Curriculum Development.

K

Koch, C. (March 15, 1996). The bright stuff. *CIO Magazine.* Available online at www.cio.com/archive/031596_qa.html

L

Larsen, S. (January 2002). *An interview with Howard Gardner. Project Zero.* Available online at www.pz.harvard.edu/PIs/HG_Larsen.pdf

M

Marcinkiewicz, H., & Sylwester, R. (November/December 2003). The brain, technology, and education: An interview with Robert Sylwester. *The Technology Source.* Available online at http://ts.mivu.org/default.asp?show=article&id=1048

Márquez Chisholm, I., & Carey, J. (Fall 2002). Information technology skills for a pluralistic society: Is the playing field level? *Journal of Research on Technology in Education, 35*(1), 58–79.

Martinez, J. (Spring 1996). Instructional design recipes. *Center for Positive Practices.* Available online at www.positivepractices.com/LearningbyDesign/InstructionalDesignRecipe.html

Marzano, R. J., Pickering, D., & McTighe, J. (1993). *Assessing student outcomes: Performance assessment using the dimensions of learning model.* Alexandria, VA: Association for Supervision and Curriculum Development.

McKenzie, J. (1999). *How teachers learn technology best.* Bellingham, WA: FNO Press.

McKenzie, W. (1998). *Walter McKenzie's multiple intelligence pages.* Available online at http://surfaquarium.com/MI/

McKenzie, W. (2004). *Standards-based lessons for tech-savvy students: A multiple intelligences approach.* Worthington, OH: Linworth.

Meacham, M. (June 2003). Using multiple intelligence theory in the virtual classroom. *Learning Circuits.* Available online at www.learningcircuits.org/2003/jun2003/elearn.html

Mitra, A., & Steffensmeier, T. (Spring 2000). Changes in student attitudes and student computer use in a computer-enriched environment. *Journal of Research on Computing in Education, 32*(3), 417–433.

Moersch, C. (2002). *Beyond hardware: Using existing technology to promote higher-level thinking.* Eugene, OR: International Society for Technology in Education.

Moersch, C. (November 2002). Measurers of success: Six instruments to assess teachers' use of technology. *Learning and Leading With Technology, 30*(3), 10.

Moursund, D. (1999). *Project-based learning using information technology.* Eugene, OR: International Society for Technology in Education.

N

National Institute for Literacy. (February 2004). *Equipped for the future: 21st century skills for the new economy.* Available online at http://eff.cls.utk.edu/PDF/eff_brochure.pdf

NETS Project. (2000). *National educational technology standards for students: Connecting curriculum and technology.* Eugene, OR: International Society for Technology in Education.

Noon, S. (October 1998). 4 stages of technology adoption: Part one—Training the pre-literate end user to use computers in the classroom. *Classroom Connect,* p. 11.

Noon, S. (November 1998). 4 stages of technology adoption: Part two—Training the software technician to use technology in the classroom. *Classroom Connect,* p. 11.

Noon, S. (December 1998–January 1999). 4 stages of technology adoption: Part three—The electronic traditionalist. *Classroom Connect,* p. 21.

Noon, S. (February 1999). 4 stages of technology adoption: Part four—Training techno-constructivists. *Classroom Connect,* p. 11.

November, A. (2001). *Empowering students with technology.* Glenview, IL: Pearson Skylight.

P

Pierson, M. E. (Summer 2001). Technology integration practice as a function of pedagogical expertise. *Journal of Research on Computing in Education, 33*(4), 413–430.

R

Rodrigues, S. (Fall 2000). The interpretive zone between software designers and a science educator: Grounding instructional multimedia design in learning theory. *Journal of Research on Computing in Education, 33*(1), 1–15.

T

Thirunarayanan, M. O., & Perez-Prado, A. (Winter 2001–2002). Comparing Web-based and classroom-based learning: A quantitative study. *Journal of Research on Technology in Education, 34*(2), 131–137.

V

Vannatta, R. A., & Beyerbach, B. (Winter 2000). Facilitating a constructivist vision of technology integration among education faculty and preservice teachers. *Journal of Research on Computing in Education, 33*(2), 132–148.

Vannatta, R. A., & Fordham, N. (Spring 2004). Teacher dispositions as predictors of classroom technology use. *Journal of Research on Technology in Education, 36*(3), 253–271.

Veenema, S., & Gardner, H. (November 1, 1996–December 1, 1996). Multimedia and multiple intelligences. *The American Prospect 7*(29). Available online at www.prospect.org/print-friendly/print/V7/29/veenema-s.html

W

Warlick, D. (2003). *Raw materials for the mind* (3rd ed.). Raleigh, NC: The Landmark Project.

Wiggins, G., & McTighe, J. (1998). *Understanding by design.* Alexandria, VA: Association for Supervision and Curriculum Development.

Williams, D. L., Boone, R., & Kingsley, K. V. (Spring 2004). Teacher beliefs about educational software: A Delphi study. *Journal of Research on Technology in Education, 36*(3), 213–229.

APPENDIX **D**

National Educational Technology Standards

National Educational Technology Standards for Students (NETS•S)

The National Educational Technology Standards for Students are divided into six broad categories. Standards within each category are to be introduced, reinforced, and mastered by students. Teachers can use these standards as guidelines for planning technology-based activities in which students achieve success in learning, communication, and life skills.

1 Basic operations and concepts

- Students demonstrate a sound understanding of the nature and operation of technology systems.

- Students are proficient in the use of technology.

2 Social, ethical, and human issues

- Students understand the ethical, cultural, and societal issues related to technology.

- Students practice responsible use of technology systems, information, and software.

- Students develop positive attitudes toward technology uses that support lifelong learning, collaboration, personal pursuits, and productivity.

3 Technology productivity tools

- Students use technology tools to enhance learning, increase productivity, and promote creativity.

- Students use productivity tools to collaborate in constructing technology-enhanced models, preparing publications, and producing other creative works.

4   Technology communications tools

- Students use telecommunications to collaborate, publish, and interact with peers, experts, and other audiences.

- Students use a variety of media and formats to communicate information and ideas effectively to multiple audiences.

5   Technology research tools

- Students use technology to locate, evaluate, and collect information from a variety of sources.

- Students use technology tools to process data and report results.

- Students evaluate and select new information resources and technological innovations based on the appropriateness to specific tasks.

6   Technology problem-solving and decision-making tools

- Students use technology resources for solving problems and making informed decisions.

- Students employ technology in the development of strategies for solving problems in the real world.

National Educational Technology Standards for Teachers (NETS•T)

All classroom teachers should be prepared to meet the following standards and performance indicators.

I Technology operations and concepts

Teachers demonstrate a sound understanding of technology operations and concepts. Teachers:

A demonstrate introductory knowledge, skills, and understanding of concepts related to technology (as described in the ISTE National Educational Technology Standards for Students).

B demonstrate continual growth in technology knowledge and skills to stay abreast of current and emerging technologies.

II Planning and designing learning environments and experiences

Teachers plan and design effective learning environments and experiences supported by technology. Teachers:

A design developmentally appropriate learning opportunities that apply technology-enhanced instructional strategies to support the diverse needs of learners.

B apply current research on teaching and learning with technology when planning learning environments and experiences.

C identify and locate technology resources and evaluate them for accuracy and suitability.

D plan for the management of technology resources within the context of learning activities.

E plan strategies to manage student learning in a technology-enhanced environment.

III Teaching, learning, and the curriculum

Teachers implement curriculum plans that include methods and strategies for applying technology to maximize student learning. Teachers:

A facilitate technology-enhanced experiences that address content standards and student technology standards.

B use technology to support learner-centered strategies that address the diverse needs of students.

C apply technology to develop students' higher-order skills and creativity.

D manage student learning activities in a technology-enhanced environment.

IV   Assessment and evaluation

Teachers apply technology to facilitate a variety of effective assessment and evaluation strategies. Teachers:

A   apply technology in assessing student learning of subject matter using a variety of assessment techniques.

B   use technology resources to collect and analyze data, interpret results, and communicate findings to improve instructional practice and maximize student learning.

C   apply multiple methods of evaluation to determine students' appropriate use of technology resources for learning, communication, and productivity.

V   Productivity and professional practice

Teachers use technology to enhance their productivity and professional practice. Teachers:

A   use technology resources to engage in ongoing professional development and lifelong learning.

B   continually evaluate and reflect on professional practice to make informed decisions regarding the use of technology in support of student learning.

C   apply technology to increase productivity.

D   use technology to communicate and collaborate with peers, parents, and the larger community in order to nurture student learning.

VI   Social, ethical, legal, and human issues

Teachers understand the social, ethical, legal, and human issues surrounding the use of technology in PK–12 schools and apply that understanding in practice. Teachers:

A   model and teach legal and ethical practice related to technology use.

B   apply technology resources to enable and empower learners with diverse backgrounds, characteristics, and abilities.

C   identify and use technology resources that affirm diversity.

D   promote safe and healthy use of technology resources.

E   facilitate equitable access to technology resources for all students.

National Educational Technology Standards for Administrators (NETS•A)

All school administrators should be prepared to meet the following standards and performance indicators. These standards are a national consensus among educational stakeholders of what best indicates effective school leadership for comprehensive and appropriate use of technology in schools.

I Leadership and vision

Educational leaders inspire a shared vision for comprehensive integration of technology and foster an environment and culture conducive to the realization of that vision. Educational leaders:

A facilitate the shared development by all stakeholders of a vision for technology use and widely communicate that vision.

B maintain an inclusive and cohesive process to develop, implement, and monitor a dynamic, long-range, and systemic technology plan to achieve the vision.

C foster and nurture a culture of responsible risk-taking and advocate policies promoting continuous innovation with technology.

D use data in making leadership decisions.

E advocate for research-based effective practices in use of technology.

F advocate, on the state and national levels, for policies, programs, and funding opportunities that support implementation of the district technology plan.

II Learning and teaching

Educational leaders ensure that curricular design, instructional strategies, and learning environments integrate appropriate technologies to maximize learning and teaching. Educational leaders:

A identify, use, evaluate, and promote appropriate technologies to enhance and support instruction and standards-based curriculum leading to high levels of student achievement.

B facilitate and support collaborative technology-enriched learning environments conducive to innovation for improved learning.

C provide for learner-centered environments that use technology to meet the individual and diverse needs of learners.

D facilitate the use of technologies to support and enhance instructional methods that develop higher-level thinking, decision-making, and problem-solving skills.

E provide for and ensure that faculty and staff take advantage of quality professional learning opportunities for improved learning and teaching with technology.

III Productivity and professional practice

Educational leaders apply technology to enhance their professional practice and to increase their own productivity and that of others. Educational leaders:

A model the routine, intentional, and effective use of technology.

B employ technology for communication and collaboration among colleagues, staff, parents, students, and the larger community.

C create and participate in learning communities that stimulate, nurture, and support faculty and staff in using technology for improved productivity.

D engage in sustained, job-related professional learning using technology resources.

E maintain awareness of emerging technologies and their potential uses in education.

F use technology to advance organizational improvement.

IV Support, management, and operations

Educational leaders ensure the integration of technology to support productive systems for learning and administration. Educational leaders:

A develop, implement, and monitor policies and guidelines to ensure compatibility of technologies.

B implement and use integrated technology-based management and operations systems.

C allocate financial and human resources to ensure complete and sustained implementation of the technology plan.

D integrate strategic plans, technology plans, and other improvement plans and policies to align efforts and leverage resources.

E implement procedures to drive continuous improvements of technology systems and to support technology replacement cycles.

V Assessment and evaluation

Educational leaders use technology to plan and implement comprehensive systems of effective assessment and evaluation. Educational leaders:

A use multiple methods to assess and evaluate appropriate uses of technology resources for learning, communication, and productivity.

B use technology to collect and analyze data, interpret results, and communicate findings to improve instructional practice and student learning.

C assess staff knowledge, skills, and performance in using technology and use results to facilitate quality professional development and to inform personnel decisions.

D use technology to assess, evaluate, and manage administrative and operational systems.

VI Social, legal, and ethical issues

Educational leaders understand the social, legal, and ethical issues related to technology and model responsible decision-making related to these issues. Educational leaders:

A ensure equity of access to technology resources that enable and empower all learners and educators.

B identify, communicate, model, and enforce social, legal, and ethical practices to promote responsible use of technology.

C promote and enforce privacy, security, and online safety related to the use of technology.

D promote and enforce environmentally safe and healthy practices in the use of technology.

E participate in the development of policies that clearly enforce copyright law and assign ownership of intellectual property developed with district resources.

This material was originally produced as a project of the Technology Standards for School Administrators Collaborative.